ARCHITECTURAL TREASURES OF EARLY AMERICA

COLONIAL
ARCHITECTURE
IN
MASSACHUSETTS

ARCHITECTURAL TREASURES OF EARLY AMERICA

COLONIAL ARCHITECTURE IN MASSACHUSETTS

From material originally published as
The White Pine Series of Architectural Monographs
edited by
Russell F. Whitehead and Frank Chouteau Brown

Prepared for this series by the staff of
The Early American Society

Robert G. Miner, Editor
Anne Annibali, Design and Production
Jeff Byers, Design and Production
Nancy Dix, Editorial Assistant
Patricia Faust, Editorial Assistant
Carol Robertson, Editorial Assistant

An
Early
American
Society
Book

Published by Arno Press Inc.

Copyright © 1977 by Arno Press Inc. and The Early American Society, Inc.

Library of Congress Cataloging in Publication Data

Main entry under title:

Colonial architecture in Massachusetts.

    (Architectural treasures of early America : v. 2)
(An Early American Society book)
    1.   Architecture, Colonial—Massachusetts.
2. Architecture—Massachusetts. I. Miner, Robert G.
II. Early American Society. III. The Monograph series,
records of early American architecture. IV. Series.
NA730.M4C68   720'.9744   77-14471

ISBN: 0-405-10065-5 (Arno)   ISBN: 0-517-53236-0 (Crown)
Distributed to the book trade by Crown Publishers, Inc.

CONTENTS

APPLYING BALSAM
WOOL INSULATION, KIND
OF WOOD, ETC.

8'-6"

4'-7¾"

PLASTER
BALSAM WOOL
SHEATHING
SIDING
2"X4" STUDS

FINISH FLOOR
1"X2" FURRING STRIPS
BALSAM WOOL
FIRST FLOOR LINE

ROUGH FLOOR
2"X10" FLOOR BEAMS
6"X8" PLATE
BOLTS 4'-0" O.C.

FOUNDATION W.

2'-4½"

4'-7¾"

GLASS 6"X6"

3'-4½"

ELEVATION·OF·WINDOW
SCALE 3/8" = 1'-0"

BRICK FIRE STOP

5½" SIDING 4½" TO WEATHER

4" X 1⅛" CORNER BOARD

PLASTER

BALSAM WOOL

⅞" SHEATHING
SIDING

MODERN·CONSTRUCTION·OF
AN 18TH·CENTURY·TYPE·HOUSE
BASED·ON·THE·WHITMAN·
HOUSE·FARMINGTON·CONN·
SCALE 3/4" = 1'-0"
DRAWN BY KENNETH CLARK

18th Century Massachusetts Architecture

OUTSIDE of that very early and almost conjectural Colony house type that at first reflected far more of the aspect of its English Gothic predecessor than it hinted at the lighter form of classical dwelling, there was also the early and unpretentious "farm-house." It was doubtless because of its simple and economical lines that this type persisted for so many years,—even, as a matter of fact, until this very day,—although its late derivatives are, unfortunately, so deficient in all its original inherent attributes of beauty of proportion and delicacy and refinement of moulding and scale as scarcely to permit the relationship to be now recognizable.

So these earlier dwellings, which were generally of the very simplest pitch-roof type,—the low shed, with its eaves hardly above the ground at the back, being in the most part a later addition,—continued to reappear, for well over a hundred years, as the houses of the "first settlers" in new communities, springing up along the New England coast and its inland river valleys. They also persisted, till a much later time, as the "farm-house" *par excellence* throughout all New England.

To cover the development thoroughly, it is perhaps necessary further to speak of the houses of the humbler families, or those built in the more sparsely settled communities, and in those sections where the men were fisher-folk or the farms sterile or sandy. Here a still simpler kind of cottage, of one story, with a low-pitched or gambrel roof, was simultaneously developing in use; but this "cottage type" is so architecturally distinct and separate a form that its consideration here would

but serve to confuse the reader interested in tracing the development of New England Colonial architecture—and so, having been mentioned, it will be left until it can be fully and separately studied by itself.

To resume, this simple pitch-roof, farm-house type, one room deep and two stories high, was at first built exclusively with one ridge pole and two end gables, making the simplest possible form of roof, unbroken by dormers, as it then provided only an unfinished attic space meagrely lighted from the gable ends. The pitch of this roof varied greatly. A few very early examples show the steeper pitch of Gothic influence. Later it lowered naturally to more nearly the Georgian proportion; though there can be no doubt but that the builders of these simple houses were more concerned to get just that exact relation where the pitch was steep enough to throw off the water from its shingled slopes, with the use of the minimum factor of safety, while it would still be low enough to permit of the use of the shortest and smallest rafter lengths allowed by a due regard for these practical requirements, than to display any regard for, or perhaps even knowledge of, the classic precedent that had then recently become customary and established in England. But the roof pitch continued gradually to flatten as time went on—a process in which the kind of roof with two slopes, known generally as "gambrel," may somewhat have assisted—until at last, well into the nineteenth century,—1830 or 1840, or thereabouts,—it arrived at the low slope appropriate to the revival of the Greek influence that, when first blending with its predecessor, produced such beautiful and dignified results.

HOUSE AT WAYLAND, MASSACHUSETTS.   Detail of Entrance.   Built about 1800.

OLD FARM-HOUSE AT MILTON, MASSACHUSETTS. Built before 1800.
An unusual element occurs in the old porch and in the projection of the first-story rooms.

But as this very simple yet beautiful farm-house type did not always satisfy the needs of those communities that were, by the end of the eighteenth century, growing decidedly more prosperous, developing a wealthy class that in their turn at once demanded more pretension and style in their dwellings while being willing and able to expend more money upon them, both the plan and the architectural style of these houses began rapidly to change. In plan the house first grew a service ell that extended more and more, as the prosperity of the farm grew, until it often ran slam into the big barn itself. This was the almost invariable method on the farm, where land was plenty and the living requirements of the family itself changed but little from generation to generation.

Detail of Entrance.
FARM-HOUSE AT MILTON, MASSACHUSETTS.
The pilasters are an excellent example of chisel carving.

Sometimes this ell grew on at the rear, sometimes it extended at the side, sometimes it grew in two parts (then generally termed "wings") extending either to right and left of the old house, or, less frequently, running back from each side or end, making the "E" shape plan.

In the Colonial village or town, however, so simple an "addition" met neither the needs nor conditions that were most likely to exist. Land was more restricted and expensive, and, what was quite as important, the growing social amenities of family life required more than the old two-room first-story plan. It is true that at first it was possible to retain one of these rooms as a parlor and turn the old dining-room into a separate living-room, building a new dining-room and kitchen at the rear in an ell. But this was merely an emergency measure, perhaps necessary in temporarily fixing over the old house. When the time to build a new one arrived, the two-room plan of the old farm-house was exactly doubled: the center hall was continued through the house and two more rooms were built at the back, one upon either side. Thus a parlor, living-room, dining-room and kitchen were provided on the first floor; and, as the need of a library or office came to be felt, the old method of adding a new kitchen in an ell was again resorted to; and once again the plan began to develop and grow in this same way, following much the same natural process, it should be observed, as Nature has herself ordained for the growth of the pollywog!

So, too, the exterior underwent changes at the same time. The double depth of the house —making it nearly square in plan—ran the old pitched roof and end-gabled ridge pole so high into the air as at once to introduce new possibilities. Either its steep pitch could be retained and the old unused attic be utilized as a third living floor—an opportunity much needed by some of the very generous families accruing to the early settlers!—or the appearance of the house could be obviously helped by again re-ducing the rafter length (a practical and economical aspect natural to these early builders), thus lowering at once both the ridge and pitch of the roof. This produced an end gable that perhaps appeared rather awkward in proportion to the Colonial carpenter's eye, trained to a steeper slope; and so he probably at once thought of the possibility of pitching his roof from all four rather than from only two sides, and the newer, more prosperous and capacious square Colonial house type was born!

Typical of the "farm-house" group is the "old red house" in Milton, now a part of the large "Russell Farm"; and while its exact date is not known, it is supposed to have been built some time before 1800, by one Nathaniel Robbins, and is distinguished from most of its associates by an unusual architectural feature in the two projecting one-storied portions occurring on both ends. Although from the outside these might seem to be later additions to an older house, internally they have every appearance of having been built at the same time as the rest of the structure. The cornice and dado finish continue around the rooms without break, while inside the room does not show the break that outside allows the corner board to continue down and the projecting ell cornice to

Photograph by Wilfred A. French

THE GENERAL PUTNAM HOUSE AT DANVERS, MASSACHUSETTS. Built about 1744.
The outer vestibule and railing are carpenter additions.

Detail of Pilaster.
THE HOOPER HOUSE AT HINGHAM, MASSACHUSETTS.

brel's upper flatter slope begins. The outside vestibule entrance, at the place indicated, is unusual; and the vestibule, while, as usual, of later date, is a good example of its kind. In fact, much of the bare appearance of this house is occasioned merely by its lack of blinds.

Another very similar example of the gambrel roof type is the General Putnam House in Danvers—in its present state representing approximately the period of 1744 (although a claim has been advanced that a portion of the house is as old as 1648). This house has, in addition to its low ell, a comparatively modern vestibule with a characteristically modern carpenter's version of a balustrade above it. This house presents as much of a contrast as is possible to the Dalton House at Newburyport. While variously dated as being built from 1750 to 1760, the photograph of this house speaks for itself, presenting an unusually spacious and generous treatment of the gambrel roof slope (now slated, while the house has a new end bay and suspiciously widely spaced columns at the entrance!). The whole design nevertheless shows much more refinement of handling than is apparent in the other example mentioned.

butt against it, both refinements displaying some evident skill and forethought on the part of the builder. The difference is made up in thickness of walls; the main house front wall being furred-in to effect this purpose, as well as to provide cheeks to take care of the inside window shutters in the window reveals.

It is impossible to give a date to the porch. Its unusually simple detail and close relation to the old extension give every assurance of its being contemporaneous, despite the fact that it is so rare a feature of Colonial work. The doorway is crude and archaic in some of its chiseled carpenter-carved decoration, but all the more interesting for that. Whether built at an earlier date or not, this house could easily pass as from twenty-five to fifty years older than the date assigned it above.

The Emery House at Newburyport, built by Thomas Coker in 1796, is an unusually clear example of the simply planned front house with the added rear ell. In this case the front part has a gambrel roof, of exactly perfect proportions, and the ell a simpler pitched roof, as is often found when the ell's narrower width brings the two rafters of the same pitch as the lower slope of the gambrel to a ridge intersection occurring at the same point where the gam-

Detail of Entrance and Pediment.
THE APTHORP HOUSE AT CAMBRIDGE, MASSACHUSETTS.
Built in 1760.

THE EMERY HOUSE AT NEWBURYPORT, MASSACHUSETTS. Built in 1796 by Thomas Coker, Architect.
A good example of the New England gambrel roof type.

THE GOVERNOR WILLIAM DUMMER HOUSE AT BYFIELD, MASSACHUSETTS.
An example of the prim New England type with fireplaces on the outer end walls.

THE CRAIGIE-LONGFELLOW HOUSE AT CAMBRIDGE, MASSACHUSETTS.   Built in 1759 by Col. John Bassell.

While similar in general scheme to the Tayloe House, the detail is of a bolder type.
The doorway may also be compared with that of the Apthorp House

The Garden Front.
THE LORING HOUSE AT OLD ROXBURY, MASSACHUSETTS.   Built in 1757 by Commodore Joshua Loring.

Commodore Loring was chief naval officer in command of the King's ships in the Colonies

The Dummer House at Byfield, near Newburyport, is a less well known example of a prim New England type, of which the Warner House at Portsmouth is perhaps the best known existing structure. As in the latter case, it frequently has the brick ends that follow naturally from dividing the old center chimney and placing the fireplaces on the end walls.

Before turning to the houses of square plan, let us look for a moment at the little house in Hingham—also of L shape—locally known as the "Bulfinch House." Local legend persists in claiming that it is formed from the upper two stories of an old house, once on Bowdoin, near Bulfinch Street, in Boston, of which the lower story had been of brick, which was taken down in 1841, and this upper part rafted down the harbor in parts on a packet, carried part way up the hill, and re-erected on its present site. The charming and unusual corner pilaster is, at any rate, excuse enough for including the house here! The sturdy simplicity of the doorway is also suggestive of Bulfinch's hands.

The house built by Commodore Joshua Loring in 1757 in old Roxbury is a rarely dignified and beautiful relic of a pre-Revolutionary mansion. The entrance was originally on the west side, where two beautiful Corinthian pilasters and capitals still show beneath a porch construction put on at this end a number of years ago. The present north doorway, opening on the garden, might, solely because of its greater

Photograph by Wilfred A. French

THE DALTON HOUSE AT NEWBURYPORT, MASSACHUSETTS. Built between 1750 and 1760.
This picture is of special interest as showing the house before its recent restoration.

THE OLD TAYLOE HOUSE AT ROXBURY, MASSACHUSETTS.   Built in 1790.

One of the best examples of a refined New England Colonial house in wood.
The porches and iron balconies, all old, are rather exceptional in treatment.

refinement, also be suspected as a possible later addition.   At the back is a separate building, designed for servants' rooms on the second floor, the lower portion serving as the old shed, with five beautiful arches, some of which are now filled in.

The Apthorp House in Cambridge is an example of the more stately type of square Colonial house plan, of which the next two or three houses mentioned are further variants.   These houses were oftentimes graced with roof balustrades, preferably along the upper roof deck. As the chimneys with this plan were normally placed on the outside wall, they also often had brick ends.   It is, in New England, the local representative of the "Westover" type that was equally representative of the South.   When built for the occupancy of a Colonial bishop in 1760, it did not include the third story now shown over the pediment in the photograph of the entrance, although it was added very soon afterward—according to one story, to serve as the slaves' quarters.   While removed from its old site, and now surrounded by college dormitories, it still appears to dignified advantage, largely because of its foreground.   It is interesting to note how superior this doorway is, in strength and decision of detail, to the similar treatment to be seen on the Longfellow House, built at practically the same time—

Detail of Garden Doorway.
COMMODORE LORING HOUSE,
OLD ROXBURY, MASSACHUSETTS.

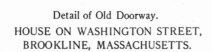

Detail of Old Doorway.
HOUSE ON WASHINGTON STREET,
BROOKLINE, MASSACHUSETTS.

16

THE ROYALL SUMMER-HOUSE
AT MEDFORD, MASSACHUSETTS.

Built in 1732.   One section still remains.

THE ELIAS H. DERBY TEA-HOUSE
AT PEABODY, MASSACHUSETTS.

Supposed to have been built in 1799
and attributed to Samuel MacIntyre.

HOUSE AT WAYLAND, MASSACHUSETTS.   Built about 1800.

THE BENNETT HOUSE AT WAYLAND, MASSACHUSETTS. Built about 1800.
Situated at the beginning of the Old Connecticut Path. This house, although late in date, is refined and delicate in treatment. The outside vestibule composes harmoniously with the rest of the design.

1759 — and of precisely similar type, standing barely three quarters of a mile away on Brattle Street. Most beautiful and aristocratic of all the New England houses of this kind, however, was the old Tayloe House in Roxbury, near the Dorchester line. Its details were notable for their delicacy and refinement, while the house, though of a regular and consistently popular plan, yet possessed minor and unusual elements, including a rounding bay and two-story porch at the rear.

An instance of a house with a lateral ell extension, although of later date, is an old house at Wayland, now owned by the architect, Mr. Ralph Adams Cram.

Detail, Entrance Vestibule.
THE BENNETT HOUSE, WAYLAND, MASSACHUSETTS.
This is a recent addition, as is generally the case where this feature is found

There happen to be two fairly well known examples of old garden houses in New England: one the summer house that, up to ten or a dozen years ago, stood back of the Royall House in Medford, on top of an artificial mound that, as a matter of fact, enclosed the old "icehouse" of the estate. While the summer house has now nearly disappeared, one section of it still remains and has been preserved with the hope of sooner or later restoring it to its accustomed site. Along with this is shown the so-called "Tea House" belonging to the Elias Haskett Derby estate, on Andover Street at Peabody, supposed to have been built in 1799 by Samuel MacIntyre.

THE PENNIMAN-STEARNS HOUSE, BEDFORD, MASSACHUSETTS
Reuben Duren, Architect

Concord, Massachusetts

THE Pilgrims landed at Plymouth Rock in 1620. Nine years later Charles the First signed the Charter of Massachusetts, and a year after, in 1630, nearly fifteen hundred men and women arrived under Winthrop and Dudley to settle upon its eastern shores. In that year, the City of Boston was settled and Watertown and Cambridge also founded.

The first inland settlement in Massachusetts was made in 1635, although it is said that it had been planned in England two years earlier; and this seems plausible from the fact that all the earliest people to settle on the site of Concord village came directly from England, and originally its only neighbors for years were "New Towne"—later Cambridge—and Watertown.

The General Court of Massachusetts issued an act of incorporation on September 2nd, 1635, for the area then known as "Musketaquid," from its Indian name, proclaiming that it "shall hereafter be called Concord." And Gov. Winthrop stated his grant was made to "Mr. Buckly and . . . ., merchant, and about twelve more families, to begin a town." The two principal incorporators were undoubtedly the Rev. Peter Bulkeley and Maj. Simon Willard; and it was placed to include the Great Fields or Great Meadows, along

the banks of the Concord River, located to the north of the Boston Road, which were immediately realized as being especially fertile.

The original area was increased by other grants. In November, 1637, the Court gave to Gov. Winthrop and his lieutenant deputy, Mr. Thomas Dudley, large additional lands bounding on the Concord River. In June, 1641, "Shawshen" was granted to Cambridge; and on Sept. 23rd, 1729, Bedford, with its sister town of Westford, were incorporated as the 25th and 26th of the fifty-nine townships finally set up in Middlesex County; Bedford's area being largely taken from Concord and Billerica—also including the whole of the area granted to Winthrop and part of the "Shawshen" or "Shawshine" grant, upon which the first dwelling had been built in 1642, and called "Shawshen House." Subsequently, both Lincoln, 1754, and Carlisle, 1757, were set off from Concord; while from Bedford, Acton was "set off" in 1684, and incorporated in 1735, Stow in 1670, and Littleton in 1715, these various townships being made up out of sections of the earliest inland townland, and new sections adjoining it.

John Duren, of the first generation in this country, settled in Billerica, possibly as early as 1659, and Reuben Duren or Durrant (the name being also

THE HILDRETH HOUSE, CONCORD, MASSACHUSETTS

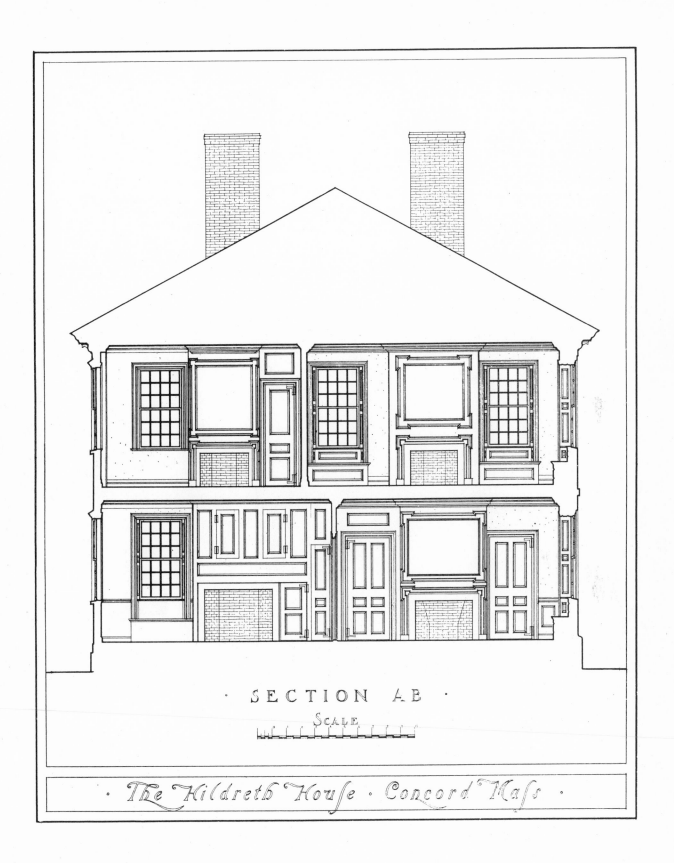

· S E C T I O N A B ·

Scale

· The Hildreth House · Concord Mass ·

spelled in other ways) was of the fourth generation. He married Mary Gould of Chelmsford on Jan. 11th, 1770, and died on Jan. 4th, 1821. He was known as "an architect and builder of first-class dwelling houses of the town" and those for Col. Timothy Jones and Rev. Mr. Penniman (now the Stearns house), pages 182 and 193, are examples—the latter being perhaps his second house in that vicinity. The Rev. Samuel Stearns was ordained on April 27th, 1796, at which time the house for his predecessor, the third minister, was not entirely finished.

In 1792 Reuben Duren purchased a tavern in Billerica, which he kept till he removed to New Ipswich, New Hampshire, where he later became famed as a builder of meetinghouses. His reputation as bridge builder, earned in Bedford, was enhanced by his model for a bridge over the Merrimac at Pawtucket Falls, which was given precedence over many competitors.

The Hildreth House at Concord, set off from all present main traveled roads, and facing out upon a quiet little triangle of green, preserves something of its original flavor of quiet dignity and comparative isolation. It would appear of about the same date as the Stearns house at Bedford from similarities of detail;

the almost direct repetition of idea shown in the two doorways; the general proportions and composition of both façades indicating, with other internal evidence, that the legend that the Hildreth house had been produced by the same designer as the Stearns dwelling is probably correct. The interiors, shown upon the measured drawing of the section, express something of the restraint, almost the inarticulateness, of many of the early New Englanders when attempting to work in the more sumptuous, freely flowing manner that seems to have come so easily to many of their contemporaries —or even to designers of somewhat earlier times—in the southern Colonies.

Deane Winthrop, a son of the Governor, was among those who signed the petition for the setting up of a part of the inland area as the township of Groton. In 1655 two new townships were authorized, Shawshin and Groton. The date of "Groton plantations" is fairly well established as between May 23 or 29, 1655.

When the line between New Hampshire and Massachusetts was surveyed and located in 1741, it was disclosed that Groton had lost to New Hampshire a large part of its area, so that there was a Groton in each state up to January 1st, 1837, when the name of Nashua was given to that portion in New Hampshire.

THE SAMUEL DANA HOUSE, GROTON, MASSACHUSETTS

Side Entrance

THE SAMUEL DANA HOUSE, GROTON, MASSACHUSETTS

DOORWAY, THE PENNIMAN-STEARNS HOUSE, BEDFORD, MASSACHUSETTS
Reuben Duren, Architect

SIDE AND FRONT DOORWAYS—THE THOMAS WHITNEY HOUSE, SHIRLEY CENTER, MASSACHUSETTS

Other portions of Groton went to make the new Pepperell, set off Nov. 26th, 1742, but not signed by Gov. Shirley until April 12th, 1753. This new township was named after Sir William Pepperell. Shirley was set off as a district January 5th, 1753, but did not become a separate township until August 23rd, 1775. Ayer was incorporated from portions of Groton and Shirley; about half of the town of Dunstable came from Groton lands, and the full tale is told with the mention that smaller parts of Groton were taken for Harvard, Littleton, and Westwood in Massachusetts, and Nashua and Hollis in New Hampshire. These several partitions left Groton finally with an area of less than half of its original forty thousand acres.

One of the older small schools in Massachusetts was in Groton, known as the "Academy," and later as Lawrence Academy, in honor of the several benefits conferred upon it by both Amos and William Lawrence of Medford, Mass. Amos Lawrence had been born and educated in Groton, and had besides served an apprenticeship for seven years in the old store of James Brazer in Groton, up to April 22nd, 1807. James Brazer was originally one of the founders of the Academy, subscribing £15 to the building fund in 1792; and so it was rather appropriate for Amos Lawrence to purchase James Brazer's house, built about 1802, and situated immediately south of and adjacent to the Academy property, and give it to the Academy in 1848. The estate of Judge Samuel Dana had been added to the Academy property in 1836; and so these two representative New England dwellings have been fortunately preserved until today, side by side upon the main road, facing out across the Meadows, being used as dormitories for the Academy scholars. During his later lifetime Samuel Dana served his district as representative in Congress, he had been president of the Massachusetts Senate, and had also served the town of Groton as its first postmaster (1801-1804).

The visitor driving through the main street of Groton today can still capture something of the village charm, from its few principal dwellings grouped closely together, with the two most imposing mansions side by side upon the higher ground that formerly looked off over the meadow farms and fields. Another fact of interest, but of no particular architectural value, except that it keys into the family record of another beautiful Colonial mansion located nearby in Woburn, relates to Loammi Baldwin, Jr., a son of the distinguished engineer of that name, who was studying law in Groton in January, 1802, when the predecessor of the Brazer House burned. Young Baldwin was boarding with Dr. Oliver Prescott, Sr., of the same family as William Prescott, who came from Groton and commanded the American forces at the Battle of Bunker Hill. He witnessed this fire and was so impressed by it, and the inefficiency of the methods then employed to fight it, that he undertook to construct an "engine" in an old shop located where the William Bruce drugstore was toward the end of the last century. This engine, known as "Torrent No. 1," was used for years in Groton, and was working in West Groton, as late as 1890, the only piece of apparatus then available in that village for the fighting of fire.

Shirley Center, the oldest section of the present township of that name, remains still largely undisturbed, partly because of its isolated position, having been left at one side when the newer automobile highway was routed through that area. It is undoubtedly for that reason that it is still possible to get much the effect of that little center of Colonial life when visiting the dwelling of Thomas Whitney, son of the Rev. Phineas Whitney, the first minister of Shirley, after its being set apart as a separate township. This occurred in 1753, on Jan. 5th; the first meetinghouse having been built in 1754. It was replaced by a second and larger structure in 1773. The cupola, was probably a part of this original building. Unfortunately, porches were added in 1804, along with other changes, and the structure was again remodeled in 1839; so that it is no longer possible to get an interesting photograph of the entire building.

Mr. Thomas Whitney, whose house remains the most important of the small group around the village, was born March 19th, 1771, and died on January 14th, 1844. We have the date of his marriage to Henrietta Parker, which was July 7th, 1799; and it is probable that his hospitable farmhouse was rebuilt a little while after that date. Standing a little back from the main street, behind its guardian elms, it is an able representative of the four-square New England type that came into being shortly before the Revolution and persisted until the more daintily graceful structures of the 1815 to 1830 period succeeded it, just before the turn to the heavy dignity of the Neo-Greek influence was to flow over the country; replacing these gracious homes with Greek temples, somewhat arbitrarily and awkwardly made to serve the purposes of a family dwelling.

The front of the house facing the Common still shows the old type shutters, lacking the middle cross style. The detail of the front porch indicates a period preceding the date of Thomas Whitney's marriage, to which some of the enlargement and additions might easily belong. The generous spacing of the front entrance porch columns, their slight, almost crude, entasis, the heavy molding of necking and base, all point to workmanship of a time much nearer the Revolution, or even somewhat preceding.

Detail of Façade
THE JAMES BRAZER HOUSE, GROTON, MASSACHUSETTS

TYPICAL HOUSES ALONG MAIN STREET, GROTON, MASSACHUSETTS

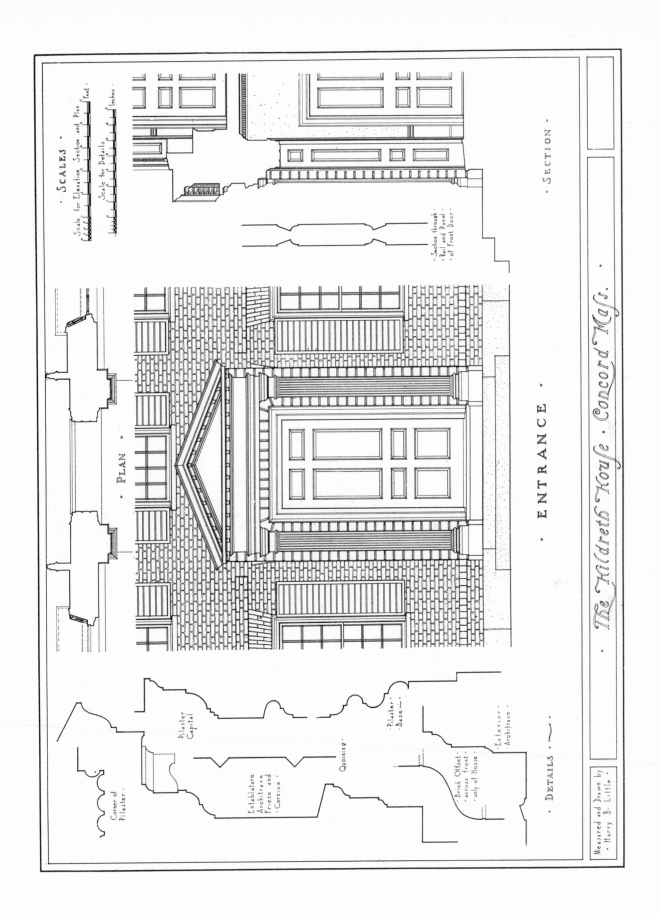

· SCALES ·

Scale for Elevation Section and Plan · Feet ·

Scale for Details · Inches ·

· PLAN ·

· ENTRANCE ·

· SECTION ·

· Section through · Rail and Panel · of Front Door ·

· DETAILS ·

· Corner of · Pilaster ·

· Pilaster · Capital ·

· Entablature · Architrave · Frieze and · Cornice ·

· Quoining ·

· Pilaster · Base ·

· Brick Offset · across front · only of House ·

· Exterior · Architrave ·

· The Hildreth House · Concord Mass. ·

· Measured and Drawn by · Harry B. Little ·

31

THE THOMAS WHITNEY HOUSE, SHIRLEY CENTER, MASSACHUSETTS

CUPOLA—MEETING HOUSE, SHIRLEY CENTER, MASSACHUSETTS

MANSION, CORNER OF MAIN AND PLEASANT STREETS,
NANTUCKET, MASSACHUSETTS.

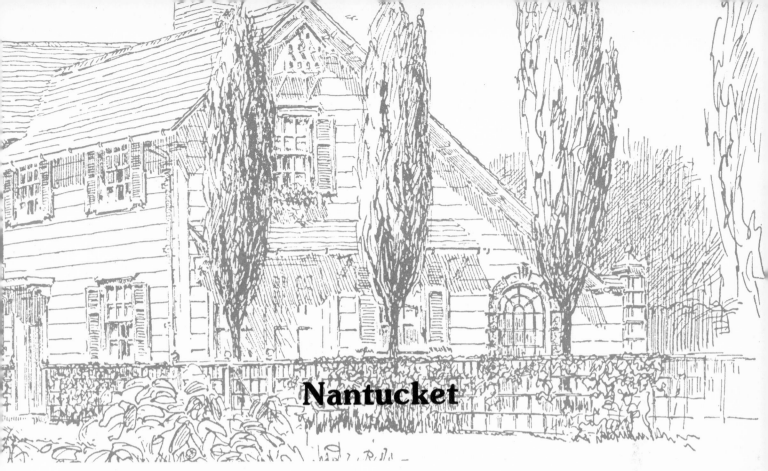

Nantucket

ON the diamond-leaded panes of the windows in a certain ancient manor house in Old England, one reads this inscription:

GOD
BY THIS MEANS
HATH SENT
WHAT I ON THIS
HOUSE HAVE SPENT

and:

ALL PRAYSE BE UNTO HIS
NAME THAT GAVE ME
MEANS TO BUILD THE SAME
1 6 3 8

This is accompanied by a couple of screws of tobacco and several pipes—indicating that tobacco did it.

On this quaint old island of Nantucket, all that is left to indicate the source of the one time wealth which built the fine old houses and mansions, are the numerous weather vanes bearing a whale, "right" or "sperm," which appear in the most unexpected places, giving an unmistakable "local color" to many a very interesting vista. There is, also, the characteristic "Captain's Walk"—a simple balustraded platform supported on posts resting on the sides of the gabled roofs, built to obtain a view of incoming and outgoing vessels. For in those days a whaling cruise often lasted years, and the homecoming was a matter of the very greatest interest to all. If one looks through the collection of the Nantucket Historical Society, and studies certain musty old volumes in Nantucket's most admirably conducted Public Library, there will

gradually emerge certain historical facts explaining the peculiar character which distinguishes the Colonial work here, from that existing anywhere else.

Nantucket was from its earliest days an Atlantic outpost far from the mainland. Its people, who were mostly English, from their very isolation became an independent, self-sufficient folk, almost a law unto themselves. More than one commission was sent from the mainland to set them right with their Colonial Governors who claimed authority over them. Quakerism was brought over from England, and from that time on the history of Nantucket is the story of the rise and fall of the Quakers. These people, so named according to Fox, the eminent English missionary of their sect, because at the mention of their Maker's name every one should tremble, were at first a simple folk, making much of personal liberty and man's natural rights, which, however, did not keep them from owning slaves both red and black; nor, while strongly advocating temperance, prevent them from taking intoxicating drinks. Adopting forms of speech designed to be a protest against caste, they did not protest against such caste. "While they ruled, it was like unto the days of Noah—all Quakers were safe within the Ark, and all outsiders were drowned in a Sea of Sin."

Many joined their church because they paid no salaries to their preachers, and their meeting-houses were of the simplest style, free from all ostentation, as were their laws; the dues, therefore, were light, and these characteristics naturally were reflected in their simple, plain architecture. It is this simplicity of form, this absence of small and enriched detail, together with a simple but well-proportioned mass, with a mastery of the "fourth dimension,"—things which did not cost a great deal of money, but which did require some expenditure of thought,—that impress one to-day as he wanders through the weed-grown streets, which are bathed in such brilliant sunlight as one gets only on a sunny day at sea; for this island is anchored thirty miles out at sea, with the Gulf Stream only sixty miles away. Standing on the boisterous beach at 'Sconset. looking over the tumultuous breakers toward the East, the nearest land is Spain.

The accompanying illustrations give clearly a suggestion of the strong clear light and deep transparent shadow on sun-flecked clapboards, cornice and doorway of many of the houses. There are the simplest expedients adopted to obtain these shadows—for example, one often finds over a door or window a seven eighths of an inch board projecting about four inches, often with no bed mould, giving just the right projection for an effective shadow. There is a cer-

tain rule-of-thumb following of Greek precedent, influenced by hands and hearts which have builded many ships; a certain tightness, of ship-shape-ness; newel posts, rails, etc., suggest the crude but strong and rugged work of the ship's carpenter. They look as if they had weathered many a salty storm and stress, and yet inexpensive—there is no ostentatious display. As Quakerism declined, and fortunes began to be made rapidly in whalebone and oil, the wealthy "Sea Captains" built more imposing mansions, such as the two porticoed houses on Main Street at the corner of Pleasant Street—two veritable classic temples in white pine—one in the Greek, the other in the Roman feeling.

In Nantucket's palmy days it ranked third in the list of the wealthiest towns of Massachusetts—after Boston and Salem. Her churches, "built out of full pockets and with willing hearts," were well filled with solid wealthy men. The Unitarians were said to be "so wealthy that they could have built their churches of mahogany, and gilded them all over."

HOUSE IN MAIN STREET, NANTUCKET.

A simple, unobtrusive, typical white house in a village street, with hardly any detail, all bathed in sparkling sunlight and splashed with purple-gray shadow; it makes a picture long to be remembered.

TWO HOUSES IN MAIN STREET, NANTUCKET.

The one nearer, the Kent House, is, all things considered, one of the best of the small houses in Nantucket, with typical doorway; it has the clean-cut, chaste effect of Greek work, and is totally devoid of all effort. The body of the house is a beautiful warm gray, the finish white; it is remarkably well kept up by a very appreciative owner.

THE GRISCOM MANSION IN MAIN STREET, CORNER OF FAIR STREET, NANTUCKET.

These were the times when Nantucket counted in the affairs of the great world. Its bold seamen, its enterprising and skilful merchants and whale hunters brought to it fame and fortune. Earlier in its history it had sent to England with a cargo of oil, etc., the two vessels, the "Beaver" and the "Dartmouth." Loaded with tea, they sailed on the return voyage to Boston, where was held the historic "Boston Tea Party." All but a very few chests of tea were thrown overboard. The remaining ones were taken by the Captains to Nantucket, and disposed of advantageously and with some discretion. This is the tradition as set forth by some of the descendants of these "Sea Cap'ns," sitting about the huge coal stove set in a circular sawdust arena, protected by a gas-pipe foot-rest, in the center of the "Captains' Room" in the ancient Rotch Building at the lower end of the Town Square. Just opposite is the very exclusive Union Club, which boasts of its works of art. And across the

Square a few steps down a quiet weedy little lane, there nestles a discreet doorway with the legend "Somerset Club" over its chaste portal.

In the rooms of the Nantucket Historical Society, among the relics testifying to this Island's past greatness, one may read the very interesting Log books of the bold whale hunters. These are often quaintly illustrated—sometimes with the number of whales taken on the day of entry, each drawn out in solid black. A few extracts from the Sea Journal of Peleg ("Pillick") Folger will give an illuminating sidelight on the character of these men. It will be inferred that "Pillick" was what is known in our times as a "good sport"—quoting consoling or congratulatory texts, according to whether the day was a profitable one or not.

"July 1st. Nantucket bears N.E. 324 miles. We had a good breakfast upon meat and doboys & we are all merry together. A

HOUSE ON ACADEMY HILL. Known as the "Captain Roland Gardner House."
A brilliant white house with deep green blinds and surrounded
with very dark green foliage, giving a very opulent color effect.

"DUTCH CAP" HOUSE IN MAIN STREET, NANTUCKET.   Known as the "Bucknam House."

THE MARIA MITCHELL HOUSE IN VESTAL STREET, NANTUCKET.

Erected in 1790.   Birthplace of the great astronomer—one of the famous women of America.   This shows a good example of the "Captain's Walk" on the roof.

DOORWAY IN QUINCE STREET, NANTUCKET.

The body of the house is a light gray with white finish. The door is of the most vivid emerald green with a brass latch; the lattice supporting a rambler rose bush and with a golden door-mat on a rose pink brick sidewalk makes a riot of brilliant color.

Doorway of the Macy House in Main Street.

slippery kind of breeze—only we wish we could get some spermaceti."

"July 8th. This day we spy'd Spermacetis & we kill'd one. If we get whale enough we may be able to go home in a fortnight. 'Death Summons all men to the silent grave.'"

"July 9th. Lat. 36–18 Longt. 73–0. Nothing remarkable this 24 hours only dull times and Hot weather & no whales to be seen. Much toil and labour mortal man is forced to endure & little profit to be got out of it."

.   .   .   .

"and we struck a large Spermaceti and killed her . . . and we hoisted her head about 2 foot above water and then we cut a scuttle in her head, and a man got in up to his Armpits and dipt almost 6 Hogsheads of clear Oyle out of her case besides 6 more out of her Noddle. He certainly doth but the right that mingles profit with delight."

And after hard weather and no whales:

"And so one day passeth after another & every Day brings us nearer to our Grave and all human employments will be at an end."

This Island during its long career suffered many disasters at home as well as in its ventures on the far seas. On a fine midsummer day in the year 1846, as usual, the coopers, spar makers, riggers, sail makers, and iron smiths were making harpoons, lances and knives, the cordage factories turning out ropes and rigging—all noisily plying their trades—the busy wharves alive with the loading of stores and unloading of cargoes of oil, and the huge drays rumbling over the cobbles with their great casks of sperm oil or huge bundles of whalebone bound for the commodious warehouses. Now the great bell in the Old South belfry booms out an alarm; the great fire which is to mark the decline of the Town's prosperity is raging. The intense heat from the burning burst the casks and hogsheads of oil, and their fiery contents spread a burning flood

Doorway of the "Bucknam House" in Main Street.

THE DYER HOUSE, No. 9 MILK STREET, NANTUCKET.

This is one of the most interesting houses in the town and is remarkable for its color and proportion. In rambler rose season there is a mass of crimson and green against a background of pinkish gray with white finish. This house is owned by some very appreciative "off-islanders" and has been kept up with a great deal of loving care.

PORCH OF THE MIXTER HOUSE ON ACADEMY HILL, NANTUCKET.

This shows, besides some peculiarly grooved detail, the remarkable decorative effect of English ivy, which flourishes well in Nantucket, and day lily leaves against a clear warm gray clapboarded house. The white pine clapboards have a suggestion of a bead on their edge.

THE MACY HOUSE IN MAIN STREET, NANTUCKET.

This is a masterly photograph by the "Official Photographer" and gives, as well as any photograph can, the atmosphere of the leafy cobbled streets and the shadow-flecked brilliance of a sunny day in Nantucket.

Entrance Porch.

THE FOLGER HOUSE IN CENTER STREET,
NANTUCKET.

over the harbor. In twenty-four hours the flames swept clean an area of thirty-six acres in the center of the Town, impoverishing more than two hundred families.

After this blow, from which the Town never recovered, the use of lard oil for illuminating began to be popular, and the recently discovered mineral oils of Pennsylvania brought a flood of oil which completely submerged the whale oil industry. So the business of whaling, in which so much of the capital of the people was invested, declined rapidly. The more enterprising men left for the mainland—some for California in the Gold Rush of '49. The last whaling ship left the port in 1869. In time, a stranded ship and a poor old widow were quoted as fit emblems of this quaint old seaport town.

Its population of real Nantucketers of about three thousand is swelled in a good season by from seven to ten thousand "off-islanders," among these being many seekers after health; its peculiar breezes which blow all day long, its sea air and its mild and fairly stable temperature of not over 82°, while on the mainland the thermometer reaches 100° and over, make it a favorite retreat for nervous invalids and seekers after sleep and rest.

The residents say that many of the fine houses were taken apart and transported by schooners to the mainland, and there re-erected—some landing in the vicinity of New York City. The white pine used almost exclusively in these houses is said by some to have come from Maine, which is not far away, by others to have grown on the Island; and they point to huge rotting stumps sometimes unearthed in certain wet places about the Island.

Most of the doors used were of but two panels —and sometimes one—the panels being in one piece often over twenty-five inches wide. In the Maria Mitchell house there is a white pine door three feet wide and six feet high and about one inch thick, painted white, made up of two pieces, one piece being twenty-seven inches wide, stand-

ing perfectly free from warping, and fitted with fine wrought-iron strap hinges, and a massive polished mahogany latch and fittings, giving to this white door an air of elegance, and all no doubt the work of some good old ship carpenter. The sashes in this house are of white pine a scant inch in thickness, with muntins one inch wide enclosing panes of glass about six inches wide by eight and three-eighths inches high; the doors, in general, being about two feet four inches wide, and fifteen sixteenths of an inch thick, of two panels in height,—so it will be seen no pine was wasted.

The interior partitions were usually not supporting partitions, the floors being carried by heavy beams mortised into heavy girts, corner posts, etc., which were exposed and painted. The partitions were, therefore, mere curtains, being made of unplaned seven eighths inch pine boards, eight to ten inches wide, with two or three inches of space between each, set vertically and nailed at floor and ceiling. In this was worked the door frame and then it was lathed and plastered on both sides, making a perfectly durable partition for such low-studded rooms—not over two and three eighths inches thick, and withal very reasonable in cost, compared with our massive two by four stud partition in these days of reckless waste. The plastering is uncommonly hard and durable. Though economical in most ways, the builders of those early days were lavish in the use of bricks, the chimneys usually being large and massive; and in the basement of old houses one often sees curious methods of brick arching and vaulting, the mortar used appearing to be a sort of light clay, crumbling to the touch, but having been serviceable for over a hundred years.

Nantucket's streets are quiet now. Many of its best houses are owned by "off-islanders" from far-away prosperous cities, who occupy them only in the vacation season. The hum of the busy shops is heard no more—and the deep rumble of the heavily laden dray with its huge hogsheads of oil bumping over the cobbled streets has given way to the rattle of the beach wagon with its summer visitors, passengers bound for the bathing beach or the melancholy ride across the somber moors, to where the huge rollers, after a journey of three thousand miles across the stormy Atlantic, break on this bleak and barren shore.

FIREPLACE DETAIL—FIRST FLOOR LIVING ROOM
THE WILLIAM HASKELL DWELLING, WEST GLOUCESTER, MASSACHUSETTS

William Haskell House

SOMETHING has already been told of the early history of the Cape Ann settlements, although not in detail. It remains a varied and confusing record. However, after three years, the first settlement of 1623 was given up. This was the Dorchester Company, whose members returned to England, except the few who followed Roger Conant to Naumkeag, and became the "Old Planters" of Salem history. Besides the temporary fish drying stages set up by the men from Plymouth, in 1624, and the brief stop of the "Talbot," en route to Salem in June of 1630, there is also the legend that the region harbored for a while the gay Thomas Morton, after his expulsion from Merrymount, near Quincy, by the more sober-minded Pilgrims.

At least two other attempts at settlement were made, in 1633, by a group under Rev. John Robinson, of Plymouth; and another "Fishing Colony," authorized in 1639, to one "Maurice Thomson, merchant." Neither succeeded; but it would appear that the region was gradually becoming populated because, in 1641, the General Court appointed a committee to "view and settle bounds" of Ipswich, Cape Ann and Jeffries Creek (later to become Manchester). This was done in February of the following year, 1642, only the year before William Haskell removed from Beverly to "Planter's Neck."

It was in 1637 that there came to the new world from Bristol, England, three brothers, all of whom at first established themselves within the area of the old Salem colony. The eldest, Roger, born in 1613, remained in Salem until his death in 1667. The second brother, William, who was born in 1617 and died in 1693; shortly after his arrival in Beverly removed to Cape Ann. The third and youngest, Mark, born in 1620, settled and lived in Beverly.

William Haskell removed from Beverly to "Glos-

ter," in 1643, when he was about 26 years old, and was married to Mary, daughter of Walter Tybbots of that colony, on November 16 of that same year. In 1645 his name is mentioned as owner of property on "Planter's Neck," a promontory lying between Lobster Cove and the ocean, on the northerly side of Cape Ann, in "Agassquam," now known as Annisquam. There he resided until either 1652, or shortly thereafter (some family histories say 1656). At any rate, on August 4, 1652, there is a record of the transfer of about ten acres, with a house and barn, from Richard Window, to Deacon William Haskell, on the west side of Walker's Creek, and the Annisquam River, in what is now known as West Gloucester.

Sometime during this early period, there appeared on the passenger list of a small vessel sailing to this colony, one Richard Window, who was there described as a "joyner." He located upon the West, or mainland, side of the Annisquam River, which even then nearly separated the Cape from the mainland. This appears to have been the same property that was later transferred, with house and barns, to Deacon Haskell in 1652. Exactly when Window built his house has not been determined, although two dates mentioned are 1645 and 1648. Even if Deacon Haskell built a new house after acquiring this property in 1652, its antiquity remains sufficiently established, and as much might still be said, if it was even built for the occupancy of his eldest son, William, after his marriage in 1667! Based upon any one of these dates, the preservation of this essential fabric, in so comparatively unchanged an estate, over all the years between, is one of those happy miracles that have occurred in only a few of our early New England structures.

The only argument against the house having been built at the earliest dates given—1645 or 1648—is that its structure proves that it was all constructed at one time, and a "two room" two-story house, in that remote location, at so early a date, seems rather pre-

LIVING ROOM LOOKING TOWARD FRONT ENTRANCE   LIVING ROOM SHOWING DOOR TO REAR LEANTO

THE WILLIAM HASKELL DWELLING, WEST GLOUCESTER, MASSACHUSETTS

OLD KITCHEN LOOKING NORTH EAST—HASKELL DWELLING, WEST GLOUCESTER, MASSACHUSETTS

tentious, when comparing it with the small "one room" Riggs cottage, across the River, for instance, which was built within a few years of 1658, one of the several hewn log houses on the Cape (and undoubtedly built with*out* benefit of instructions from the Delaware Swedes!). Yet Richard Window, as the "joiner" for the Colony, might well have chosen to express his skill in his own dwelling, even at so early a date and in the comparative isolation of its site.

The original structure—still easily to be distinguished from the two principal additions that now adjoin its outer walls—had the usual early plan, of two rooms upon each floor, each side of a large central chimney, with the staircase to the upper story built against the chimney front. The house faces south, and is but thirty-six feet front by eighteen feet deep. Each story is about 7' 5" high, from the floor to the under side of the single thickness of boarding forming the floor above. The later plaster ceilings fortunately preserved the old vermilion color that had been used at some earlier time to pick out the slightly-moulded lower edge of the beams over the larger room a treatment that has been repeated up and down the chamfered edges of the heavy oak corner posts in this same room.

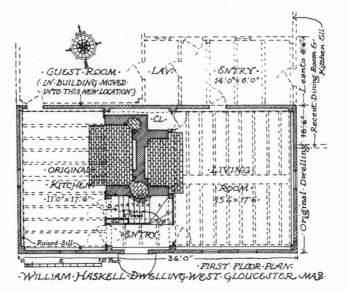

·FIRST·FLOOR·PLAN·
·WILLIAM·HASKELL·DWELLING·WEST·GLOUCESTER·MASS·

In summer time, despite its location near a main highway, the house is so protected by the trees along the brook, that it is approached in apparent isolation over a narrow dirt roadway that at first discloses only its old front, unaltered since the old casement sash were exchanged for double-hung windows early in the Eighteenth Century, and the roof and outer wall faces, which have required occasional renewal from time to time.

The present entrance door is a replacement. Within its simple framework, with old boards and still older bosses, the door itself, hung on old wrought iron angled strap hinges, and graced with a wooden bolt upon its inner face, is one of the several successful additions made by the present owners, Mr. A. H. Atkins, a well known sculptor, and his wife. Shortly after acquiring the house, Mr. Atkins was so fortunate as to find an old box containing enough old handmade

iron bosses (which had apparently never been used) to complete the illusion of authentic antiquity for this entrance that the house deserves.

To avoid making any changes in the old structure, Mr. Atkins moved up against the back of the dwelling, upon one end, an old shed upon the estate, and made its interior over into a bedroom, building a new chimney at its northern end, in which he copied one of the old fireplaces from the front house. There was also a simple shed-like structure extending eastward from the rear portion of that end of the dwelling, containing a minute kitchen that, with the entry in the leanto, provided a small dining space and lavatory off the Guest room. Within the last few years (indeed, since the major number of these pictures were taken) this end has been replaced with a somewhat larger wing containing a Dining room, as well as a Kitchen, and, in the second story, another bedroom and a couple of small baths to serve that room, as well as the old East Bedroom, from which it is unobtrusively entered, from an old closet space between. By these means, the owners secured for themselves all needed modern conveniences, and a larger capacity for the dwelling, without in any way injuring its exterior appearance, or disturbing the restful interior character of its older nucleus.

Entering, as most people do, through the door opening from the old stable yard into the leanto along the back of the dwelling, the early note is struck immediately by the few simple early chairs and table set along this miniature gallery, and the fine collection of pewter shown upon the open shelves of the small cupboard against the rear wall of the old house. This entry is plastered after the old fashion, exposing the hand-worked wooden principal timbers in the ceiling and at the corners of the space enclosed.

From this room you step down—over the old raised sill of the original house—into the larger, or Living, room of the dwelling; although it contains the smaller fireplace, as the other first story room, to the west, was the old Kitchen or Hall, with its wider, deeper and higher fireplace, containing an inner corner baking oven and warming niche. But the East Room is

THE WILLIAM HASKELL DWELLING, WEST GLOUCESTER, MASSACHUSETTS

LIVING ROOM—GENERAL VIEW LOOKING TOWARD NORTH EAST—HASKELL DWELLING,
WEST GLOUCESTER, MASSACHUSETTS

OLD KITCHEN—SHOWING DOOR TO GUEST ROOM ELL—HASKELL DWELLING

SECOND STORY PASSAGE LOOKING TOWARD
SPINNING ROOM

a very little more pretentious—if indeed, the word
can be used at all in reference to so simple an entity
as this Haskell dwelling—with its delicately edge-
moulded hewn oak beams, the shaped and chamfered
cornerposts, and the simple toothed moulding over
the fire opening, and below the inclined feather-edged
panelled boarding that extends from the old fire-lintel
to the chimney girt above.

In the front Entry, more spacious than usual for
so small a plan, the plainest possible flight of steep
stairs rises back of the single thickness of feather-
edged boarding, exposed on both faces. Between this
and the uncovered brick face of the chimney, the
flight rises from winders at the start, to a narrow
space before the door of the West chamber, probably
the Spinning Room, just wide enough to allow a per-
son to turn and pass across to the large East chamber,
at the other end of the main house.

As in most early structures, the building was probably left entirely unfinished inside its framed and
boarded walls. The simple boarding separating the
front stairs from the entry, and finishing the fireplace
room-ends, was then entirely consistent with the exterior walls. In other examples of this period, the
outer wall boarding sometimes extended continuously

for two stories, from sill to plate, relieved only by
shallow "shadow moulding" along the exposed inner
edges. The difficulties of obtaining plaster from old
Indian shell heaps caused chimneys and fireplaces to
be laid in puddled clay, as was here done, and the
few finer natural lime deposits—when found—were
reserved for lime washes or plaster wall bases. It was
rarely wasted on room ceilings.

This completes the original dwelling, but still gives
no suggestion of the beautiful and completely appropriate outfitting that the old place has so sympatheti-
cally received from its present owners. For that suggestion one must turn to the accompanying pictures,
in which have been recorded a small portion of the
many compositions that exist to delight the eye, in
whatever direction one turns, anywhere within the
structure. For not only are its occupants appreciative
of the dwelling, but they are also appreciative—and
have been acquisitive, as well!—of all the early types
of furnishings for which it supplies such unique and
appropriate backgrounds.

In one room after the other, one finds old house-
keeping equipment of the period—and of the several
generations of the old family that followed (for four
generations, at least, the "eldest son of the eldest
son" was a William Haskell). The rooms are crowded

ENTRY—FIRST FLOOR—LOOKING INTO OLD KITCHEN

LIVING ROOM LOOKING NORTH WEST—THE HASKELL DWELLING, WEST GLOUCESTER, MASSACHUSETTS

GUEST ROOM—SOUTH END WITH DOOR TO OLD KITCHEN

LEANTO GALLERY LOOKING TOWARD EAST END
THE WILLIAM HASKELL DWELLING, WEST GLOUCESTER, MASSACHUSETTS

BED ROOM OVER OLD KITCHEN—LOOKING NORTH WEST

BED ROOM OVER LIVING ROOM—LOOKING NORTH WEST

THE WILLIAM HASKELL DWELLING, WEST GLOUCESTER, MASSACHUSETTS

OLD KITCHEN—WALL OPPOSITE FIREPLACE

OLD KITCHEN—SHOWING DOOR TO FRONT ENTRY

THE WILLIAM HASKELL DWELLING
WEST GLOUCESTER, MASSACHUSETTS

with early impedimenta; old iron and wooden fittings, cranes, trammels and trammel hooks; iron trivets, skillets, pots, kettles, candlesticks, and dogs; foot stools, shovels, tongs, and coal pinchers; wooden trenchers, pewter porringers, plates and bowls. Early glazed slip-ware, or pewter and wooden mixing bowls, are near at hand, with early oak, hickory and maple or pine chairs; tables, benches and stools set handily beside the fireplace or across the room. Even wall rack pipe holders, pine knife boxes, etc., are there.

The pieces of early glass are less conspicuous, but

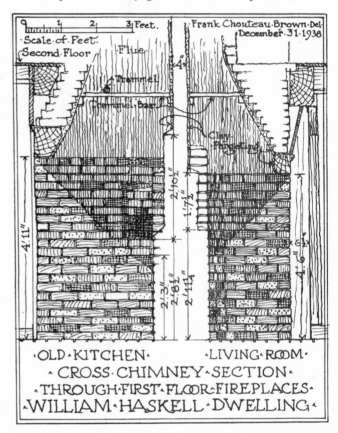

·OLD·KITCHEN· ·LIVING·ROOM·
·CROSS·CHIMNEY·SECTION·
·THROUGH·FIRST·FLOOR·FIREPLACES·
·WILLIAM·HASKELL·DWELLING·

they, too, are grouped thereabouts, as needed, along with appropriate textiles, simple hooked rugs, slight small print sash curtains, and woven bedcovers. Even the Guest Chamber in the attached shed-ell, is fitted as finely and beautifully as the more authentic rooms. In fact, the whole structure and its contents, as it stands, composes as complete and perfect a "museum" of early *Americana* as now remains in New England representative of its date and time. In proof thereof we tender for the reader's delectation some few of the many glimpses of these interiors and their furnishings, such as the painstaking craft and skill of a descendant of the younger brother of the first William Haskell now makes possible!

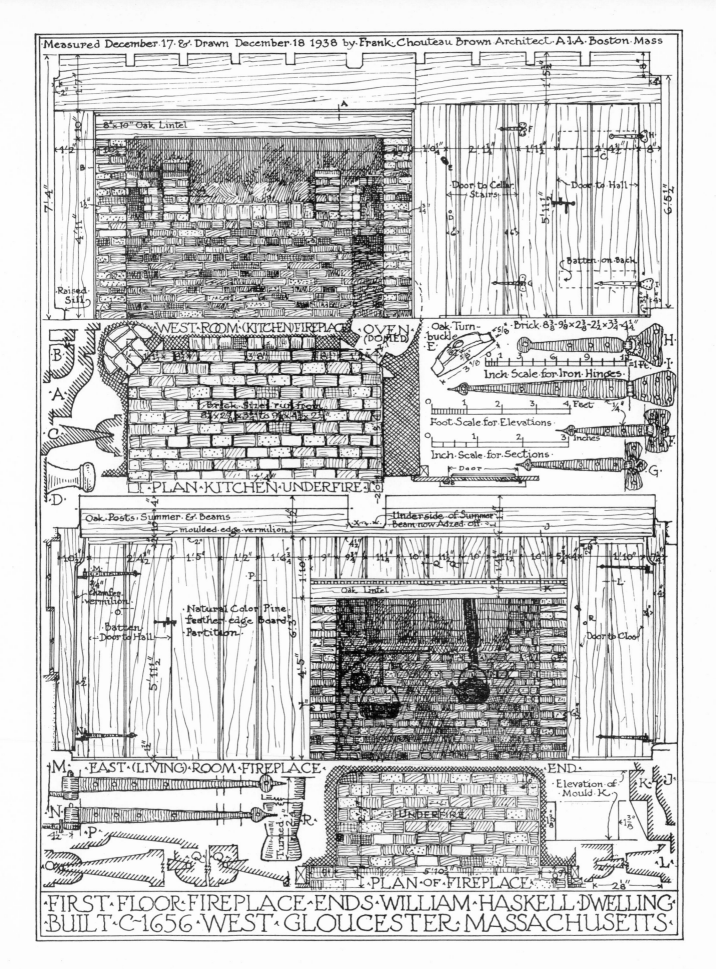

Measured December 17. & Drawn December 18 1938 by Frank Chouteau Brown Architect A.I.A. Boston Mass

8"x10" Oak Lintel

Raised Sill

Door to Cellar Stairs

Door to Hall

Batten on Back

WEST·ROOM·(KITCHEN)·FIREPLACE·   OVEN (DOMED)

Brick Size run front
8"x2⅛"x3⅜" to 9¼"x4⅛"x2¼"

Oak Turn-buckle

Brick 8⅜-9⅛ x 2⅜-2½ x 3¾-4¼"

Inch·Scale·for·Iron·Hinges.

Foot·Scale·for·Elevations.

Inch·Scale·for·Sections.

Door

·PLAN·KITCHEN·UNDERFIRE·

Oak Posts, Summer & Beams
moulded edge vermilion

Underside of Summer Beam now Adzed Off.

Oak Lintel

chamfer vermilion

Natural Color Pine feather edge Boards Partition.

Batten Door to Hall

Door to Clos?

·EAST·(LIVING)·ROOM·FIREPLACE·   ·END·

Elevation of Mould K.

Turned

UNDERFIRE

·PLAN·OF·FIREPLACE·

·FIRST·FLOOR·FIREPLACE·ENDS·WILLIAM·HASKELL·DWELLING·
·BUILT·C·1656·WEST·GLOUCESTER·MASSACHUSETTS·

PORCH OF HOUSE AT 380 ESSEX STREET, SALEM, MASSACHUSETTS
SAMUEL McINTIRE, ARCHITECT

Salem, Massachusetts

S we have already seen, Salem was the first town to be settled within the district covered by the Charter given to the members of the Massachusetts Bay Company by King Charles the First. Nevertheless, upon the arrival of the first group of settlers engaged under this Charter, who had been forwarded from England by the Governor and Members of the Company, under the command of Captain John Endecott, they found Mr. Roger Conant, and several others, already established in residence upon the land sloping down to Salem Harbor.

When Edward Winslow went back to England from the Plymouth Colony in 1623-4, he secured from Lord Sheffield a charter to "fish, fowle, hawke, truck, and trade" on "Cape Anne," and immediately on his return to Plymouth on the "Charity," in March of 1624, the ship was reladen with material and some Plymouth men and sailed to set up the "Great House," the frame of which had been prepared in England, along with the required fishing "stages," and begin the fishing and trading venture on Cape Ann.

This did not prove very successful, and Roger Conant, who was then at Nantasket, was asked to go to the Cape and take charge, in the interest of the Dorchester Company. This was late in 1624. In 1625 the Dorchester Company dissolved; but, encouraged by letters from Rev. John White of Dorchester, England, Roger Conant and a few followers withdrew to

a "fruitful neck of land in Naumkeag," where setting up their houses and planting land crops, they waited the promised reenforcements, which finally arrived under Capt. John Endecott, in June of 1628, supplanting Roger Conant. But on June 12, 1630, Endecott was supplanted in turn by the arrival of Gov. John Winthrop, in the "Arbella," which was the first of four vessels which had sailed from the Isle of Wight, on April 8; the others being the "Jewell," arriving June 13; the "Ambrose," arriving June 18; and the "Talbot," on July 2. Governor Winthrop was accompanied by Sir Richard Saltonstall, Lt. Gov. Thomas Dudley, Rev. George Phillips, and a number of others.

Meanwhile, Endecott had the "fayre dwelling" on Cape Ann "shook" and brought down to Naumkeag (now re-named Salem in honor of the peaceful arrangement arrived at between the "Old Planters" and the New) and reassembled again upon the westerly part of his lot, which lay between Washington, Federal, and St. Peter's Streets, facing Washington Street. By this arrangement the "Old Planters" were given house lots together along the line of the present Essex Street.

The Rev. Francis Higginson, who arrived with about two hundred settlers in June of 1629, speaks of a "faire house newly built for the Governor," elsewhere also described as "of the model in England first called Tudor, and afterwards the Elizabethan," and as having two stories with a sharp pitched roof.

Endecott removed to Boston in 1665, and died in 1666, his wife following him about 1678, and his house

The Capt. Joseph Waters House—1806-07

ENTRANCE DETAIL, NUMBER 29 WASHINGTON SQUARE NORTH,

WASHINGTON SQUARE— NORTH—SALEM, MASSACHUSETTS

had entirely disappeared in 1684. In 1682, part of the Endecott property was sold to Benjamin Hooper, who built upon it a "single room house," two stories high; which structure is undoubtedly the south-easterly portion of the present Hathaway House, which was removed in 1911 to the grounds beside the John Turner House ("House of the Seven Gables," on Turner Street, overlooking the Harbor). The *only* uncertainty is as to whether or not Benjamin Hooper incorporated the Gov. Endecott dwelling into the new house he was building in 1682! If that *was* done, the portion of the Hathaway House mentioned would go back to 1624, and probably to the West of England for its origin,— and so would be the oldest house frame existing in this country! The elaborate design of one of the posts is shown in the detail sketch. It is unlike any other post remaining in New England and has the peculiarly mellow yellow tone of old English oak. Miss Emmerton treats very fairly of the history of this and the adjoining houses in her book, "The Chronicles of Three Old Houses." As to the importation of the frame from England, early records of other trading settlements (even that of "Charlton"—now Charlestown—nearby) indicate it was quite customary to send out the frame of a large house—usually called "the Great House"—for the temporary common housing of all the group employed upon the venture.

Turning now to the John Turner House next door, we may deal with more definite and tangible facts. John Turner built his house—the first portion of it—

THE ROPES MEMORIAL—ABOUT 1719—ESSEX STREET, SALEM, MASSACHUSETTS

CHESTNUT STREET,
SALEM, MASSACHUSETTS

THE CAPT. RICHARD DERBY HOUSE—1762—NEAR THE HEAD OF DERBY WHARF,
SALEM, MASSACHUSETTS THE OLD COUNTING HOUSE AT THE LEFT OF PICTURE

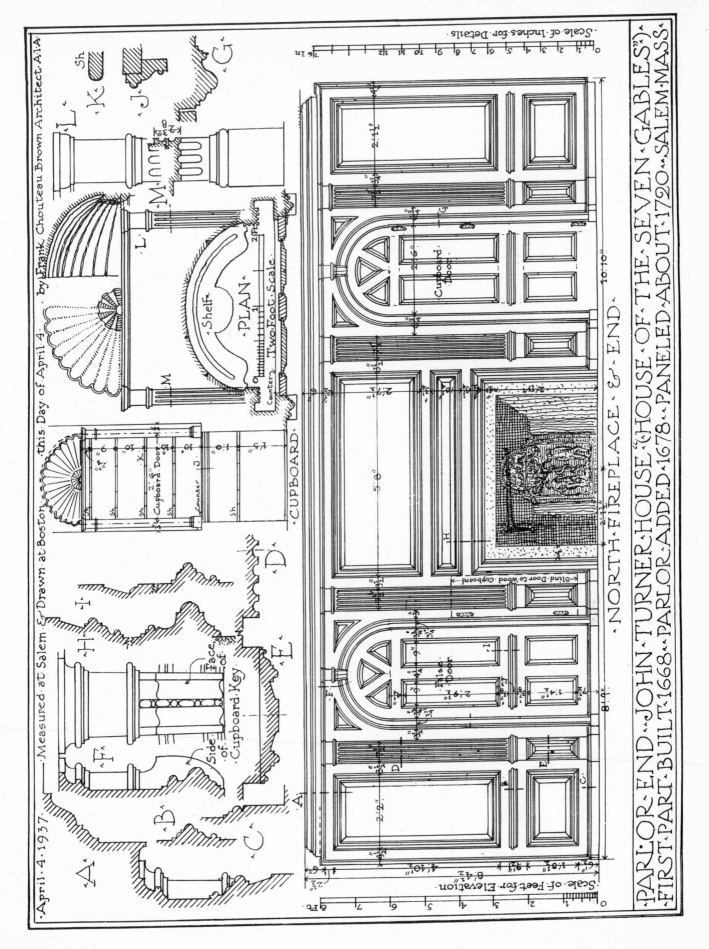

·April·4·1957· ──Measured·at·Salem·&·Drawn·at·Boston── this·Day·of·April·4· ·by·Frank·Chouteau·Brown·Architect·A·I·A·

·Scale·of·Inches·for·Details·

·L· ·K· ·J·
Sh
·M·
2⅜

·Shelf·
·PLAN·
·Counter· ·Two·Foot·Scale·
2·Ft.

·CUPBOARD·

·Cupboard·Door·
·Counter· J
6
10
2'·6"·Door
Sh
Sh
Sh
15
3

Face·
of·
Side·
of·
·Cupboard·Key·

·A· ·B· ·C· ·D· ·E· ·F· ·G· ·H· ·I·

·NORTH·FIREPLACE·&·END·

·Cupboard·Door·

·Blind·Door·to·Wood·Cupboard·

·First·Door·

·Scale·of·Feet·for·Elevation·

·PARLOR·END··JOHN·TURNER·HOUSE·("HOUSE·OF·THE·SEVEN·GABLES")·
·FIRST·PART·BUILT·1668··PARLOR·ADDED·1678··PANELED·ABOUT·1720··SALEM·MASS·

The South-easterly Portion thought to be Gov. Endecott's Dwelling erected in 1624

THE HOOPER-HATHAWAY HOUSE—1682—SALEM, MASSACHUSETTS

THE JOHN TURNER HOUSE—1668—"HOUSE OF THE SEVEN GABLES"—TURNER STREET, SALEM, MASSACHUSETTS

THE PINGREE HOUSE—1810—ESSEX STREET, SALEM, MASSACHUSETTS
Samuel McIntire, Architect

THE COOK-OLIVER HOUSE—1782—FEDERAL STREET, SALEM, MASSACHUSETTS

SAMUEL McINTIRE, ARCHITECT

in 1668. At that time he purchased the land, with a "single house" upon it (a house with one room upon each floor, and two and a half stories high, with a large chimney—and stairs in front of it—at one end), which he took down and rebuilt—possibly using part of the old frame—with the "Hall," or living room, upon the west side of the chimney and the kitchen upon the east. The house then had four gables; two upon the front and one at each end (as in the John Ward House, 1684, back of the Essex Institute). The original "Hall" is the present Dining Room. Shortly after, in 1678, the large south wing, with parlor and bedroom over it was built, with higher ceilings and roof than in the original building. At this time, too, the entrance must have been extended to the south on both floors.

Up to this time the interior of the house had probably been walled with wide pine boards, with "shadow moldings" along both edges, covering the timbered frame, which was nogged with brick laid up in clay, and daubed upon the face between the "half-timber" construction of the structure. About 1720 John Turner (the son) improved his dwelling by replacing the original casements with double hung windows, and covering the old frame and walls with plaster and the very fine panelwork that the dwelling now displays.

With the Narbonne House, built before 1671, on Essex Street, nearby, the John Ward house, and the Seven Gables group, the visitor to Salem may obtain an excellent idea of the type of Seventeenth Century architecture that prevailed in New England during

THE PIERCE-
JOHONNOT-
NICHOLS
HOUSE—1782
—FEDERAL
STREET,
SALEM,
MASSACHUSETTS

SAMUEL McINTIRE,
ARCHITECT

STABLES AND
COURT YARD

the years of its settlement. This understanding may be further strengthened by a visit to the "Pioneer Village" in nearby Forest River Park,—where some early Puritan houses and Colonial industries were set up for the Salem Tercentenary celebration.

Following these Seventeenth Century houses, Salem also presents a group representative of the early part of the succeeding century. Of these the Ropes Memorial, built about 1719, is most easily available to visitors, and contains exceptional fittings and furnishings, with a nice old garden behind a fine fence, at the side.

The earliest brick house in Salem is the Derby House, built in 1762 by Capt. Richard Derby, near the head of Derby Wharf. Its beautiful paneled interiors, and the old wooden Counting House beside the doorway, may be incorporated into the Permanent Memorial, with famous Derby Wharf restored, and the Federal Custom House of 1819 nearby. Besides this, an earlier but little known Custom House, built in 1805, also exists off Essex Street.

But after all, Salem is better known for its architecture of the later and more elaborate period, when Samuel McIntire and his associate carvers were in their prime. During the years that brought about "the turn of the Century" into the Eighteenth, Mr. Samuel McIntire was as much in demand in Salem as was Bulfinch in Boston.

While Chestnut Street contains some of the best houses of the late Salem period, in summer they are mostly obscured by the thick foliage of beautiful trees, that do much to add charm and appeal to that stately avenue,—and the houses bounding on Washington Square, in another—and less regarded—part of the town, are also among the most imposing in the city.

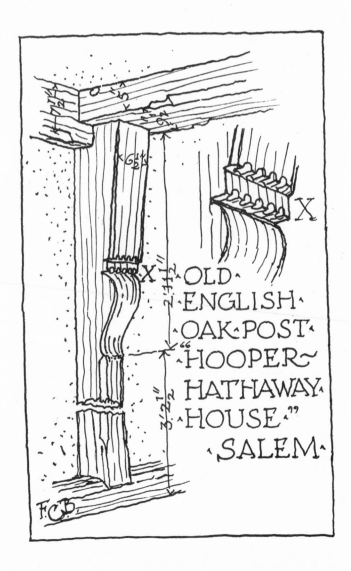

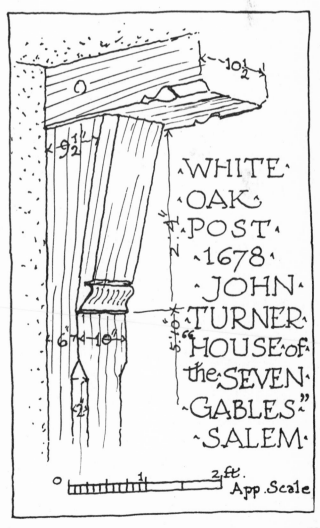

THE ELIAS ENDICOTT PORTER FARMHOUSE—1737—LOCUST STREET, PUTNAMVILLE, DANVERS, MASSACHUSETTS

Danvers, Massachusetts, Part I

S TEMMING, as the township of Danvers does, so directly from the Salem settlement, it follows that much of its early beginnings already has been disclosed. It was one of the many townships that were later set apart from the area originally established, as within the Naumkeag (later to be known as the Salem) settlement. As they exist today, Danvers includes a portion of the land that was the original "Salem Village," or "Farms"; which also then included most of the present area of Peabody, which lies between Danvers and Salem to the south and east.

Beverly and Wenham also extend along its eastern side, with Wenham and Topsfield on the north; and Topsfield and Middleton on the west. All these townships also were included in the original Salem, with the addition of Manchester and Marblehead, although it only included a part of Topsfield. Indeed, the original grant, given by "the Council for New England" to Endecott and the Dorchester Company included most of Essex County—and parts of Norfolk, Suffolk and Middlesex, as well!

Later, in 1629, the Charter of King Charles the First, gave to "the Governor and Company of the Massachusetts Bay in New England" power for its "freemen" to elect annually their own Governor, Deputy, and eighteen Assistants—who made up "the Great and General Court," with authority to establish laws over the new settlement. It was true that a "freeman" had to be also a member of the established church, in good and regular standing, but, when it was discovered that these elections had been taken over by the settlers themselves (whereas it had evidently been originally intended that the electoral government would be handled altogether by the English members of "the Company"); it was arranged—after fifty-five years of operation—to substitute another charter, with rather less liberal terms, for the earlier document of the Council for New England.

Peabody remained a part of the Danvers area until 1855, when it became a separate township. It had formerly been known as Brooksby. And Danvers did not secure its full and complete independence as a township, even in 1752, when, after a long struggle for separation from Salem, it was granted separate town government. But only as a "District" without individual representation in the General Court.

Although the first profitable industry of the Salem settlement was fishing, it was not long before a large part of this business was taken over by the Marblehead community and about Salem Harbor there gradually developed the more profitable business of maritime merchandising on the larger scale available at the time, until the town's piers and warehouses were soon handling the products of the ports of all the world. But, meanwhile, there was also the need of growing the farm produce necessary to maintain the daily life of the settlement, and it was soon discovered that the region about the Harbor was none too fertile, and the land none too well adapted to this purpose. And so Salem Village—or "the Farms"—became the farming center of the settlement. There, on land adjacent to the Harbor, to the north and west, was much rich soil disposed upon gently rolling hillsides and fertile valleys, and more protected from the sometimes boisterous winds and storms along the seacoast.

Gov. John Endecott had in 1632 been granted by the General Court, a large farmstead for himself in what is now Danversport, in recognition of his services to the Colony. He called it "Little Orchard Farm" and a part of the original property was still owned by the late William C. Endicott, at the time of his death a year or two ago. Governor Endecott ordered fruit trees from England and by 1640 had planted a large orchard, of which the famous "Endecott Pear Tree."

In fact, three early grants comprised most of the present areas of Danversport and Peabody. Besides the Endecott lands, these included the grant to the Rev. Samuel Skelton, (made in July, 1632) and that to John Humphrey (1635) which extended nearly to

THE ELIAS ENDICOTT PORTER FARM—1737—LOCUST STREET, PUTNAMVILLE,
DANVERS, MASSACHUSETTS

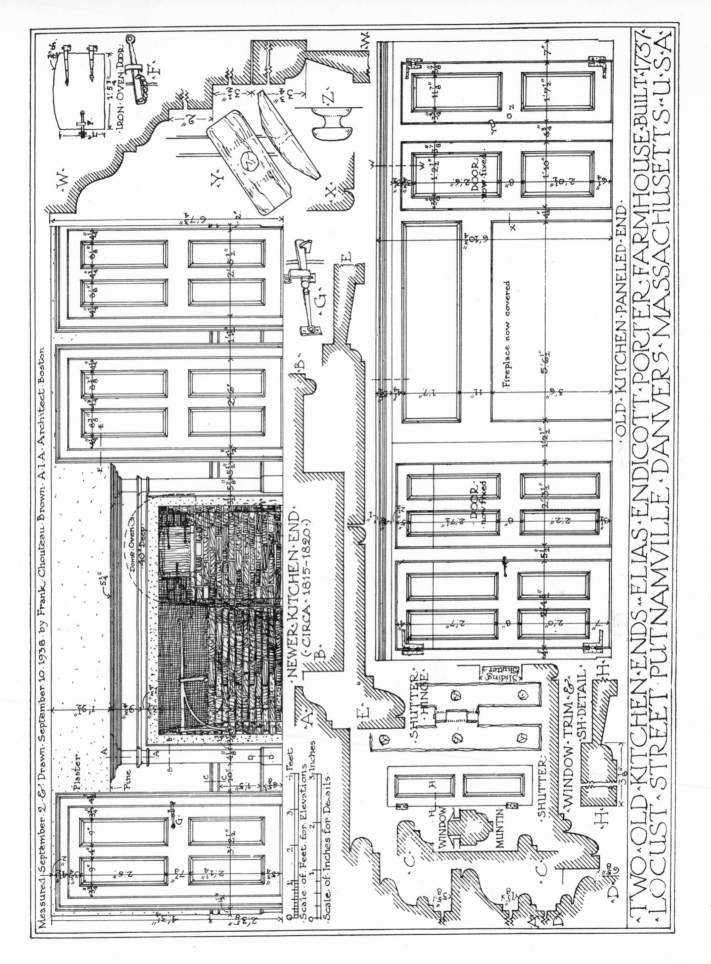

TWO·OLD·KITCHEN·ENDS··ELIAS·ENDICOTT·PORTER·FARMHOUSE·BUILT·1737·
LOCUST·STREET·PUTNAMVILLE·DANVERS·MASSACHUSETTS·U·S·A·

·OLD·KITCHEN·PANELED·END·

·NEWER·KITCHEN·END·
·(·CIRCA·1815-1820·)·

Measured·September·2·&·Drawn·September·10·1938·by·Frank·Chouteau·Brown·A·I·A·Architect·Boston

Scale·of·Feet·for·Elevations

Scale·of·Inches·for·Details

·IRON·OVEN·DOOR·

Fireplace now covered

DOOR· now fixed·

DOOR· now fixed·

Dome·Oven·40″ Deep

Plaster·

Pine·

·SHUTTER·HINGE·

·SHUTTER·

·WINDOW·TRIM·&·SH·DETAIL·

·SLIDING·SHUTTER·

·WINDOW·

·MUNTIN·

73

the Lynnfield boundary. From 1635 on, many additional interior land grants were made to those families who wished to carry on farming in the community. Thus, by 1638 there was a well-defined separate settlement in the "Village" or "Farms" area, first established under the Rev. John Phillips, who later returned to England. These later grants of farm lands were all made by the Salem selectmen, including one (made about 1640) to John Putnam—whose family name has since become indissolubly associated with the history of the town, as well as that of the Commonwealth and the Country during the Revolution. About 1644 another grant of some 300 acres was made to John Porter, in "Danvers Plains," and he was later credited with establishing the first tannery.

After several petitions to the Salem fathers, in 1672 the "Salem Village Parish" was allowed to be organized. This included Danvers — outside the "Port" — about half of Peabody, and a part of Beverly. The word "Parish," as used in this connection meant rather a "town" than a "church," so that from that time on until 1752, when Danvers was finally "set off" from Salem, the parish records actually were the records of the town.

In 1673 was built the first Meeting House, a structure of 34 x 28 feet, on a site that has been identified as in a field now near the corner of Hobart and Forest Streets. The old "Training Field" for the militia company organized in 1671, was the "Common" at Danvers Highlands, given to the town in 1709 by Deacon Nathaniel Ingersoll. A few years later, in 1676, a "Watch House" was erected on "Watch House Hill," an eminence about at the "Highlands" parsonage pasture, although the Church in this section was not organized until 1689.

In the "Witchcraft Delusion," which flourished in Salem Village in 1692, the First Village Meeting House—which was also used as the "Town House"

THE GEORGE JACOBS HOUSE
DANVERSPORT, MASSACHUSETTS

of the community was employed for the "examination" of some of the victims—and it may have been partly to help forget this regrettable hysteria that a new Meeting House was begun in 1700, on "Watch House Hill." It was a structure that has been described as nearly square in plan (the dimensions having been 48 x 43 feet) and built at a cost of 330£. It had a hip roof of the rather steep pitch of the period, a "tower" or cupola story rising from the centre of the roof, and interior galleries. It continued in use until 1752 and was finally demolished in 1786. In 1710, the "Middle Precinct" was given permission to build its own church; and by 1711 a new Meeting House, 51 by 38 feet, had been constructed. The contributing area included what is n o w known as Peabody and a part of Middleton (which was not set apart until 1728), then k n o w n as "Mills Hill." Finally, in 1752, the "District of Danvers" was incorporated, but without being given the privilege of a delegate to the General Court. The town records show that at that time there were 25 slaves living within the new "District" limits.

In connection with the "Witchcraft Delusion," there remain three structures in which dwelt individuals whose names were associated with its history. The Sarah Prince-Osborn House, 1660, now at 273 Maple St., but formerly on Spring St., has been both moved and remodelled. Sarah Osborn was among the first accused, was tried on March 1, and died while in Boston Jail the following May. Rebecca Nurse was the fourth woman accused by Tituba, a West Indian slave of the Rev. Samuel Parris, minister of the Salem Village church, in whose household the delusion originated. Rebecca Nurse was then seventy years old, and lived in an old house off Pine St., built in 1678, which was rather too thoroughly "restored" in 1909; but which nevertheless still provides a good popular idea of the appearance of a seventeenth century dwelling. She was hanged July 19, 1692, and her body placed

VIEW OF NORTH SIDE SHOWING "LEAN-TO" AT REAR

VIEW OF REAR AND WEST END

THE REBECCA NURSE HOUSE—1678—DANVERS, MASSACHUSETTS

Measured August 27 & Drawn August 28 1938 by Frank Chouteau Brown A.I.A.

Foot Scale for Drawing

Inch Scale for Details.

Reeding Soffit Y.

Pilaster W.

20 Reeds on Face →

Reveal 2¾

4½" O.C.

6¼ Y

X

V

3"

V

8"

5¾ 6" 8"

Z

10"

4½

W

9¾ 5¾ 3'2" 5¾ 9¾

5'9"

2¾

1'8"

11"

5'9½"

1'6"

9½" 2½"

3⅞

7⅝"

9¼"

Sawn out
Pattern in
Soffit at X.

Scale

·ENTRANCE· DOORWAY· HOUSE· OF·
SAMUEL PUTNAM·1812·DANVERS·MASS

76

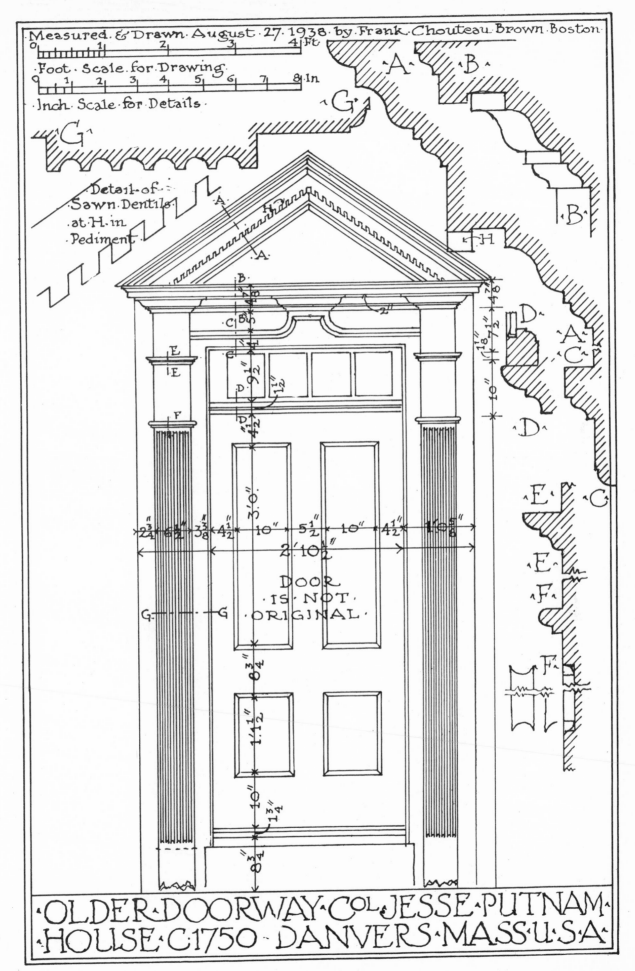

Measured & Drawn August 27 1938 by Frank Chouteau Brown Boston

Foot Scale for Drawing

Inch Scale for Details

·G·   ·A·   ·B·

·G·

Detail of
Sawn Dentils
at H in
Pediment

·A·

·A·

·H·

·D·
·A·
·C·

·D·

·E·
·C·

·E·

·F·

·F·

DOOR
IS NOT
ORIGINAL

G——————G

2' 10½"

OLDER·DOORWAY·Col·JESSE·PUTNAM·
HOUSE·C·1750·DANVERS·MASS·U·S·A·

77

THE SAMUEL PUTNAM HOUSE, DANVERS, MASSACHUSETTS

THE JAMES PUTNAM HOUSE—DANVERS, MASSACHUSETTS

THE JESSE PUTNAM HOUSE, DANVERS, MASSACHUSETTS

in the family burying ground, now to be found in a field near some pines off Collins St.

The third, the George Jacobs House, is now in process of disintegration, having been abandoned several years ago after a fire that damaged one end. Jacobs was tried and hanged on August 19, 1692. The remains of the Jacobs house, built about 1658, may still be seen in a field overlooking Waters' River, looking out toward the Beverly shore to the east, and the

cerned with its occupancy by Gen. Thomas Gage, the last Provincial Governor of Massachusetts, during 1774, just previous to the Revolution. He resided at "The Lindens," a fine house built for a summer residence by Robert ("King") Hooper of Marblehead, in 1754, and a room in the Col. Jeremiah Page House, a narrow gambrel dwelling built about 1754 and formerly facing on Danvers Square, (but now removed to 11 Page St. for the headquarters of the Danvers

OLDER PART AT REAR—1648. FRONT PORTION ADDED 1744
THE GENERAL ISRAEL PUTNAM HOUSE—DANVERS, MASSACHUSETTS

original "Little Orchard Farm" of Governor Endecott, with the three-story Reed-Porter House to the west. Even in its final stages it displays the sturdy construction of its time, with the heavy pinned framework, brick nogged, still resisting the untimely results of its exposure to the weather through all the years.

Another principal association of this area is con-

Historical Society), for his office.

But probably the name most generally and widely associated with the town of Danvers is that of the Putnam family of Revolutionary fame, of whose houses there still remain a large number in this township. The two doorways measured for this issue, (from the Col. Jesse Putnam and Samuel Putnam

THE COL. JESSE PUTNAM HOUSE—C. 1750—DANVERS, MASSACHUSETTS

REAR WITH "LEAN-TO" AND VESTIBULES

DETAIL OF FRONT, "THE LINDENS"—1754—FORMERLY AT DANVERS, MASSACHUSETTS

"THE LINDENS"—1754—FORMERLY AT DANVERS, MASSACHUSETTS

houses) show an early and a late example, of which the latter displays a few typical details and mouldings found repeated in many other houses in the vicinity.

Danvers also provides several examples of "double" houses, one being the Col. Jesse Putnam Farmhouse (1750), a short distance beyond which is the Joseph Putnam house, where Gen. Israel Putnam was born, near the old Newburyport turnpike. The older part (1648) of this latter house is at the rear, there having

two more rooms, added across the rear of the older portion; the whole still being enclosed by a wide gambrel rather than merely a "lean-to," in order to secure two full-height rooms across the rear upon second floor.

The Elias E. Porter Farmhouse on Locust Street, although having a flat sloping roof with end gables, also grew to its present size in exactly the same way; by the same first three steps of enlargement. To that outline, however, some owner also added a "semi-

SOUTH EAST ROOM ON FIRST FLOOR
THE JAMES PUTNAM HOUSE—DANVERS, MASSACHUSETTS

been a newer portion (added in 1744) built entirely across the front toward the street.

The James Putnam house (which is located about midway between the two other houses of the same family just mentioned, but a little way from the main highway), gained its present sizeable gambrel by degrees. It was probably first a two-story "one-room" house; then widened by the addition of another room, adding to the width of its front. Later, the old narrow gambrel was heightened and widened to cover

lean-to" extending partly across the rear of the house, and a finely proportioned end vestibule. The northern end of this house has the unusual fenestration of five narrow fifteen-light windows on both the first and second floors, and this farm at one time boasted twenty-seven buildings! Much of the interior detail dates from its later enlargement (probably about 1810 to 15) and is of unusual delicacy, while it also displays many of the characteristic local details so evidently favored by Danvers builders.

84

THE ELIAS ENDICOTT PORTER FARMHOUSE—1737—LOCUST STREET, DANVERS, MASSACHUSETTS

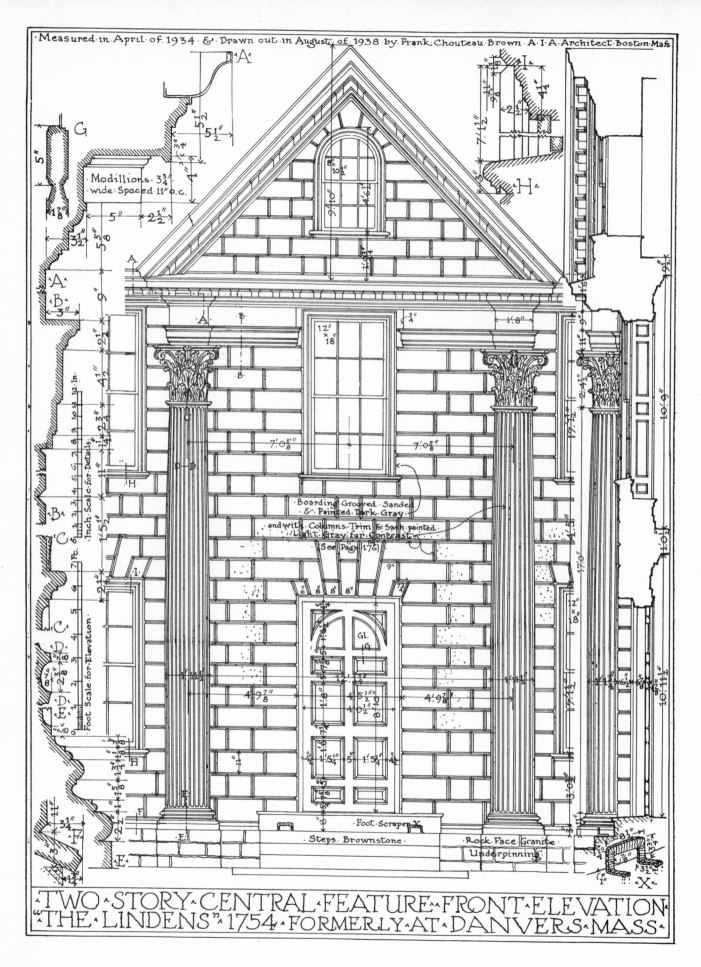

Modillions 3¾″ wide Spaced 11″ o.c.

Boarding Grooved Sanded & Painted Dark Gray
and with Columns Trim & Sash painted
Light Gray for Contrast
(See Page 176)

Foot Scraper X

Steps Brownstone

Rock Face Granite Underpinning

Inch Scale for Details
Foot Scale for Elevation

·TWO·STORY·CENTRAL·FEATURE·FRONT·ELEVATION·
"·THE·LINDENS·"·1754·FORMERLY·AT·DANVERS·MASS·

Danvers, Massachusetts, Part II

OVER most of the area of early Salem ("Naumkeag") not much original structural work remains. Business has of recent years pretty well supplanted many old buildings over large sections of what is now the more populous part of Salem, Beverly, and Peabody. Then, twenty-four years ago, there was the "Salem fire," that swept away a large residential area of that center and the waterfront almost up to the Custom House and Derby Wharf locations—the latter now in process of rebuilding by the Federal Government. We must turn, therefore, to the former less-built-up region of "The Farms," to find the greatest number of local examples of dwellings built previous to the Nineteenth Century, as well as those that are perhaps less well-known and less familiar to the casual visitor, or even, to the usual student.

So, leaving Salem—as well as the seaside margins of Marblehead and Beverly—and turning inland toward the west, and north, and skirting the shores and inlets of Beverly Bay upon the right, one today still follows the ancient highway from Salem to Danvers and Danversport.

After passing the Jacob's House location in the fields on the right, and the three-story Read-Crowninshield-Porter dwelling at Danversport upon the left, just before the roadway makes a sharp right-angle turn, near the head of the inlet from Beverly Harbor, are the "twin houses," side by side, overlooking Crane River inlet and the old shipyard sites, built by Captains John and Moses Endicott, probably dating from about 1798.

Beyond the center—and rather different from any other example of dwellings within the old Salem area—is the house built about 1784 by the Rev. Benjamin Wadsworth, near the old parsonage site, now Centre Street. While not exactly a common type in New England, it is nevertheless, in its sturdy and vigorous detail, and in the somewhat unusual combination of hip-and-gambrel roof lines, a form of dwelling that indubitably belongs to the period of the Revolution,

or within the short decade following.

After passing "The Mills" and Danvers Square, both north and west the agricultural character of this region has been well maintained over all the years between its original settlement and the present date. The oldest structures are to be found along some of the older roads, or down rutted lanes and driveways, where old groves of trees and clustering overgrown shrubs suggest the location of early dwellings to one experienced in such a quest. Even then one meets many disappointments; for far too many of the old sites have been usurped by later buildings, or the old house—if it is still to be traced at all—has been surrounded by newer ells and additions, and often entirely rebuilt to suit the requirements of more recent owners. Such a Danvers house was "Oak Hill," for instance, set far back from the road, in mid-Victorian ugliness, but yet containing the remnants of an older dwelling; including two rooms by Samuel McIntire, that now fortunately have been transplanted to a more accessible and safer location in the Boston Art Museum. As the building had been sold to be adapted to other purposes, this removal, at least, was justified.

Less happy was the fate of "The Lindens." Built as the country place of the Hon. Robert (better known as "King") Hooper of Marblehead in 1754, it was—in its chosen setting of gardens, and linden-planted approach—a noble example of a fine New England dwelling of the period. Its dignified design and finish, high ceilings, and rooms with four-paneled walls, marked it as one of the best in all that countryside. But it fell upon evil days. It was purchased as a gamble by second-hand furniture dealers. It was up for sale, piecemeal or wholesale, over several years. One fine interior went to a Middle Western museum. The room paneling was cheaply reproduced and (so rumor hath it) sold again! And, finally, a purchaser for what remained was found; and now the site shows only the remains of the trees and the old garden—and a gaping cellar hole! The dwelling has been re-erected upon a closely crowded urban lot in a semi-southern city,—far from "its own, its native land" with much of its glamour and glory reft ruthlessly away!

"The Lindens" formerly on Sylvan Street, on land that was part of the original Endecott grant and sometimes known as "The Governor's Plains," had a stairway that was second in beauty and spaciousness only to that in the hallway of the Lee Mansion in Marblehead; and the first and second hall wall covering was also reminiscent of the treatment that may still be seen in the Marblehead Mansion. But in its exterior design, the gambrelled Danvers dwelling possessed an unusual façade; having a central feature, with two engaged Corinthian columns and steep-pitched pediment along with four richly-moulded dormers and a decorative roof balustrade.

The house was purchased from the Hooper heirs in 1797—a few years after its builder's death—by Judge Benajah Collins, related to the local Eppes family; whose farm, now in Peabody, was purchased by Elias Haskett Derby of Salem, and developed as his summer estate by Samuel McIntire. It was here that the charming, unusual two-story summerhouse was built at the cost of 100£ and completed by McIntire in July, 1793. In 1901, it was moved four miles across country, and has since that time decorated the Endicott gardens at Danvers and combined the favorite "archway" feature—employed so frequently by McIntire to focus the vista beyond a garden approach—upon the lower story, with diminutive rooms on either side, from one of which rises the stairway to the upper floor, which provided a summer Garden Room to overlook gardens and pleasance on all four sides. The pilastered second story is surmounted by a pedimented roof treatment, with two Watteau-like carved figures, and corner pedestals with finely turned vases—the whole most exquisitely and delicately proportioned and scaled.

"THE LINDENS"—FORMERLY IN DANVERS, NOW IN WASHINGTON, D. C.

THE JUDGE SAMUEL HOLTEN HOUSE, DANVERS, MASSACHUSETTS

There were also three McIntire mantels that—at some injury to the original paneling—were somewhat arbitrarily incorporated by Francis Peabody into "The Lindens," when he owned the place in 1860; two from his grandfather's house in Salem, and one from "Oak Hill," added in 1873. The two McIntire mantels from the Joseph Peabody House were placed in the room at the right of the entrance on the first floor, and in the bed-room on the right at the head of the stairs. The mantel from "Oak Hill" was located in the northwest bed-room on the second floor. It was during his occupancy that the gardens also were extended somewhat to the west.

It is, of course, customary, when quoting a date for an old building, to give that of the oldest part known to have been located upon the site. Often that portion first built was but as large upon the ground as a single room, facing toward the south, with a large fireplace and constricted staircase upon one or the other end.

The structure was often two stories and attic high; sometimes only a story and a half cottage. In either case, the easiest and most obvious first enlargement of its size was to add to its length, thus making full use of the original stairs and chimney, for both old and new rooms, upon both floor levels.

As in the case of this dwelling the various additions have been fairly definitely determined, and although there still remains some doubt as to the exact years in which each addition was made, it illustrates this "progressive development" which can be suspected —and sometimes traced—in many other old New England dwellings. The portion first built, probably erected by Benjamin Holten (also sometimes spelled "Houlton"), about 1670, was a typical "one-room-house plan," with one room on each of two floors, and an attic, and a large chimney and stairs at the southwest end. The first addition was made about 1689, and consisted of another room adding to the

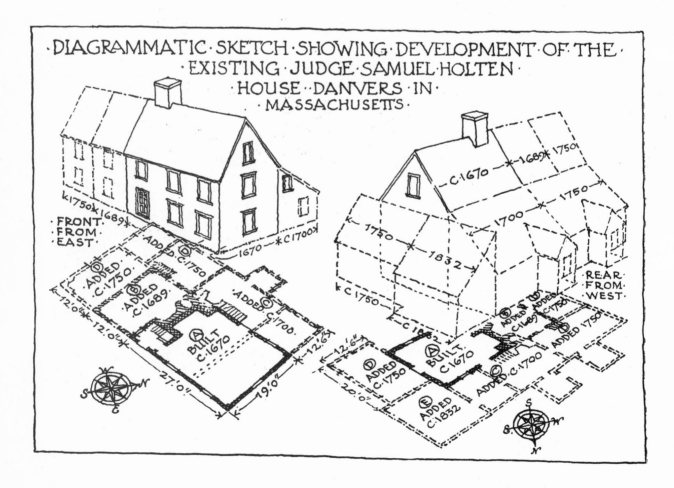

DIAGRAMMATIC·SKETCH·SHOWING·DEVELOPMENT·OF·THE· ·EXISTING·JUDGE·SAMUEL·HOLTEN· HOUSE·DANVERS·IN· ·MASSACHUSETTS·

90

THE JUDGE SAMUEL HOLTEN HOUSE, DANVERS, MASSACHUSETTS

structure's length, upon the other side of the chimney and stairs. But instead of being as large or even, as was most usual, a little larger than the earlier room —the new room was smaller and of less width upon the front. This extended the roof ridge and the front of the house about twelve feet more to the southwest.

The next addition (the second) was also made in the usual way, in about 1700. It was the regular "lean-to" at the rear. Again it was not *quite* the usual thing,—as it only extended as far as the original "one-

the end gable house wall, extending beyond the front wall of the dwelling, to shelter an outside door and make a short "Beverly jog." This room was probably intended to provide Judge Holten with an office; and it may have been a few years apart from the extension to the southwest, in which case it might have been the fourth addition made to the original plan!

Again, in 1832—or thereabouts—another room was added in the indented north corner of the house; and probably the front vestibule was made, by moving

ENTRANCE HALL AND STAIR
THE JUDGE SAMUEL HOLTEN HOUSE, DANVERS, MASSACHUSETTS

room" portion, and the roof was established at a slightly flatter slope than that upon the main house. The third addition was made about fifteen years later, when the building was largely rebuilt, perhaps in 1752. It consisted of another room on the southwest end, (again adding about twelve feet to the length of the house front and to its ridge) and the extension of the rear "lean-to" at the same time, while another "lean-to" was built against the northeast end, but to quite different effect, as here the roof sloped up against

out the old front door and adding another beside it, at about the same time. These last changes were made after the death of its most famous occupant, Judge Samuel Holten, in January, 1816, when he was 78 years old.

He had been a member of the State Provincial Congresses of 1768 and 1775; a member of the General Committee of Safety; representative of Massachusetts at the Yorktown Convention of 1777, when he helped in framing the "Articles of Federation"; President of

THE JUDGE SAMUEL HOLTEN HOUSE, DANVERS, MASSACHUSETTS

4'-7" x 6'-10" x ⅞" Door

View of Stair Hall

THE SAMUEL FOWLER HOUSE—1809—HIGH AND LIBERTY STREETS, DANVERS, MASSACHUSETTS

VIEW ACROSS ENTRANCE HALLWAY

SOUTH WEST ROOM, FIRST FLOOR

THE SAMUEL FOWLER HOUSE—1809—HIGH AND LIBERTY STREETS, DANVERS, MASSACHUSETTS

THE SAMUEL FOWLER HOUSE—1809—HIGH AND LIBERTY STREETS, DANVERS, MASSACHUSETTS

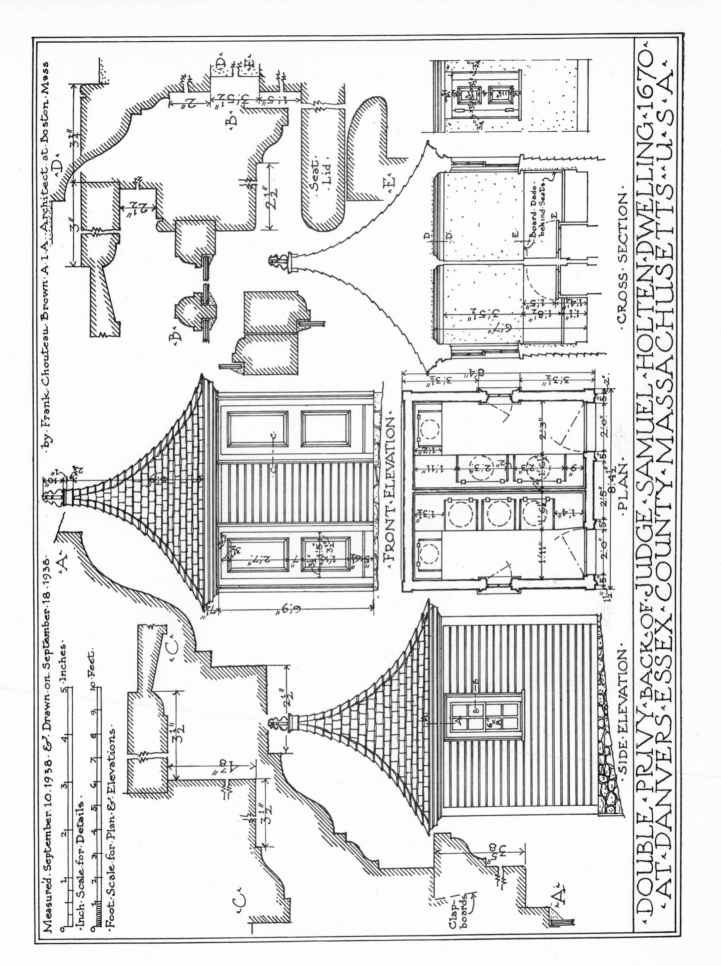

· Measured · September · 10 · 1938 · & · Drawn · on · September · 18 · 1938 ·

· Inch · Scale · for · Details ·

· 5 · Inches ·

· Foot · Scale · for · Plan · & · Elevations ·

· 10 · Feet ·

· by · Frank · Chouteau · Brown · A · I · A · Architect · at · Boston · Mass ·

· CROSS · SECTION ·

· FRONT · ELEVATION ·

· PLAN ·

· SIDE · ELEVATION ·

Seat Lid.

Board Dado behind Seats

Clap-boards

· DOUBLE · PRIVY · BACK · OF · JUDGE · SAMUEL · HOLTEN · DWELLING · 1670 ·
· AT · DANVERS · ESSEX · COUNTY · MASSACHUSETTS · U · S · A ·

97

the Continental Congress in 1785; 32 years Judge of Essex County Court of Common Pleas; 35 years Judge of General Sessions, for 15 of which he was acting Chief Justice; also occupant of many honored positions in the town—selectman, moderator, treasurer, etc., and served five years in the State Senate and twelve years on the Governor's Council.

He left his house to his daughter, Mary Putnam, and his granddaughter, Mary Ann Putnam; and it is

and Liberty Streets, is a fine example of New England restraint in material and design. Built at a period when, especially in this locality, local builders and ship-craftsmen had developed a large number of delicately-worked variants of ornamental wood mouldings, its selection of material had largely eliminated this type of ornament and fallen back instead upon sheer, chaste beauty of proportion and composition. So this dwelling can be accepted as perhaps typical of

SIDE VIEW ACROSS YARD
THE SAMUEL FOWLER HOUSE—1809—DANVERS, MASSACHUSETTS

probable that the "double" vestibule and privy date from about that time, or perhaps a little later, in 1823.

Samuel Fowler, born 1776 and died 1859, built the simple square brick house known by his name, in 1809. His father had owned and conducted a shipyard at the "New Mills"; and he continued as mill owner, as well as operating a large tannery near Liberty Bridge. This dwelling, on the corner of High

the severely simple type of brick dwelling architecture of that period, of which elsewhere within its limits the same township furnishes several other, although smaller, instances of structures employing the same material and a nearly similar simplicity of design.

It is now among the several structures owned by the Society for the Preservation of New England Antiquities, representing different cultural periods, and is one of the most consistently perfect of them all.

Both in its architecture and furnishing it is of a simplicity that seems quite *un*architectural in all its means. Not the least of its appeal to the appreciative student is the number of original wall papers that have been preserved upon its rooms, including one scenic paper decorating the Parlor.

This paper is believed to have been among the first printed by Jean Zuber et Cie, who while still using many small wood blocks for the many colors of their

which was immediately accepted and has continued in use until today.

The painted designs of the wall decorations in the Hall and principal rooms of the Lee Mansion, in Marblehead, were made upon sheets of paper about 26" x 22". This work in style recalls French *grisaille* painting, while the Classic forms employed in the design also suggest French decorators or, possibly, English copyists as their origin. The other wall coverings

Near the Old Parsonage Site, Now Centre Street
THE WADSWORTH HOUSE—C. 1784—DANVERS, MASSACHUSETTS

patterns, were the first to combine these printings upon continuous rolls of paper to be applied perpendicularly. Previously all wall paper printings had been made upon squares of paper usually about 15" x 19" to 18" x 22". Then these were separately pasted upon the wall to make up the panel of the design. The change was made by Zuber about 1829 and its obvious convenience and saving of time in application made it an advance in the manufacture of wall paper,

in the Fowler House are of more conventional pattern and simpler coloring, of which the coldly Classical or Adam-like character of that on the Hall is perhaps unusually successful in striking the identical note in decoration that is to be discerned in the architectural restraint of the exterior, in the precise, yet attenuated mouldings of the staircase, mantels and, indeed, of all the woodwork of the interior, as may be seen in the photographic views reproduced herewith.

GARDNER-WHITE-PINGREE HOUSE—
1804—SALEM, MASSACHUSETTS
DETAIL OF MANTEL IN FRONT DRAWING ROOM

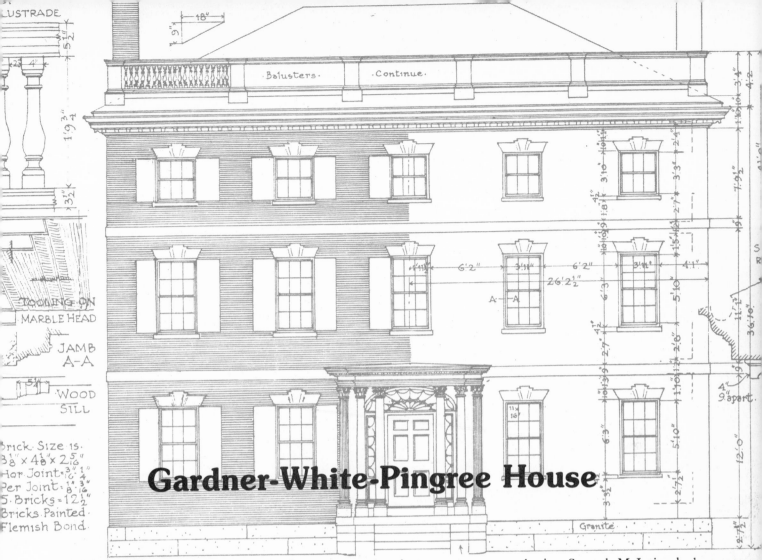

Gardner-White-Pingree House

Labels visible in drawing (architectural annotations):
- BALUSTRADE
- Balusters. Continue.
- TOOLING ON MARBLE HEAD
- JAMB A-A
- WOOD SILL
- Brick Size is. 3⅛" × 4⅛" × 2⁵⁄₁₆" · Hor Joint 3'0"·¼" · Per Joint 8'3"·⅛" · 5 Bricks = 12½" · Bricks Painted · Flemish Bond
- A - A
- 26'2½"
- 6'2"
- Granite
- 9' apart

Gardner-White-Pingree House

AMONG the artisans of New England the name and fame of Samuel McIntire has spread far beyond the local boundaries of his native town of Salem, Massachusetts. Although probably best known as a carver of wood, he is also to be credited with the actual design of many of the mansions in and about Salem, with which his name is still associated—and while his abilities as a designer were not—in his early years—commensurate with his skill as a woodworker, among his later structures may be found examples of a refinement and perfection in treatment that are not to be bettered by any among his contemporaries.

His father, Joseph McIntire, was also a "Housewright," or carpenter—as we would term him today. Samuel was born January 16, 1757, and had two brothers, both of whom were also trained in his father's shop, and later assisted Samuel to complete many of the houses of local McIntire fame—thus considerably extending the period of years and number of houses with which the name could be associated!

His elder brother, Joseph, later became his principal assistant. He was born nine years before Samuel, and still another assistant—his younger brother by two years—was Angier. Samuel McIntire had also a son, Samuel F. McIntire, who assisted his father; as was also true of the sons of his elder brother, Joseph. So, actually, we have the name of McIntire associated with the buildings of Salem for a period of three generations, or probably about seventy-five years, including the working years of his father! Samuel himself died in 1811, but left behind him many drawings and designs, as well as the large school of relatives and assistants who had been helping him.

Early in life he bought a house at 31 Summer Street, Salem, in which he lived, and built his shop in the rear of the dwelling. This house was built in 1780, and as Samuel McIntire's best known early house is the Pierce-Johannot Nichols Mansion, which was started in 1782, he must from the first have been very successful in business. Despite the delicacy of his carvings and their design, his early buildings were over-bold and of heavy relief—of which this house provides an excellent example. Later, his style of design became more refined, but remained somewhat ornate and still "heavy" in character—as in the Cook-Oliver dwelling, perhaps—and it was not until his later years, that he acquired the experience and feeling that made possible the simplicity and distinction

FRONT FAÇADE AND ENTRANCE PORCH
GARDNER-WHITE-PINGREE HOUSE—1804—SALEM, MASSACHUSETTS
Samuel McIntire, Architect

that is to be found in the David Pingree House.

This dwelling—lately known as the Gardner-White-Pingree House, and numbered 128 Essex Street—fortunately has been preserved through its acquisition by the Essex Institute, and is representative of McIntire's third and best period. The sheer simplicity of this house façade is characteristic—the relation of story above story, with only a slightly-projecting band of marble to mark the floor lines between; the windows set almost flush with the wall face, and no other ornament except the flush marble lintels and the charmingly naïve porch, up to the cornice and eaves

balustrade above! But lack of pretentious detail is compensated by its perfect scale and the proportion of all its parts. Those who desire more elaboration may turn to the interior, where equal restraint, along with great delicacy of carving, ornaments the mantels, staircase, door frames, and cornices throughout.

The interiors have been very carefully furnished from the collections of the Essex Institute and others. As a result, some rooms are simple and dignified, while others are definitely more gay and provocative in their color schemes and draperies.

The Dining Room conforms to the first classifica-

DETAIL OF ENTRANCE PORCH

tion, with simple blue-toned wall, and Venetian blinds. The two rooms on the eastern side are more frivolous. The front room windows have simple draped underpieces of plain gauze or muslin, with parti-colored fringe, re-echoing the sprigs of embroidered, flowering sprays on the draped muslin overpiece. The rear room has a similar window material, all in white, with white embroidered sprays. In both rooms the walls are covered with a strong yellow paper, plain in the front room, and with panels of classical subjects breaking up the width in the rear Parlor. In both, a classical frieze goes above the dado, and a narrow band below the cornice, with a vine edging the wall openings— all printed in shades of blue.

The second floor front room draperies are peachblow silk, with a peach and blue-striped similar material festooned above the hangings. A similar arrangement of this material forms the posted bed canopy. The bedroom at the rear has blue watered silk at the windows and pale tinted walls. The larger west room has a light blue tinted plaster wall, with an East Indian damask with rosebuds, blue cords and tassels at the windows, and the bed is covered with blue brocade.

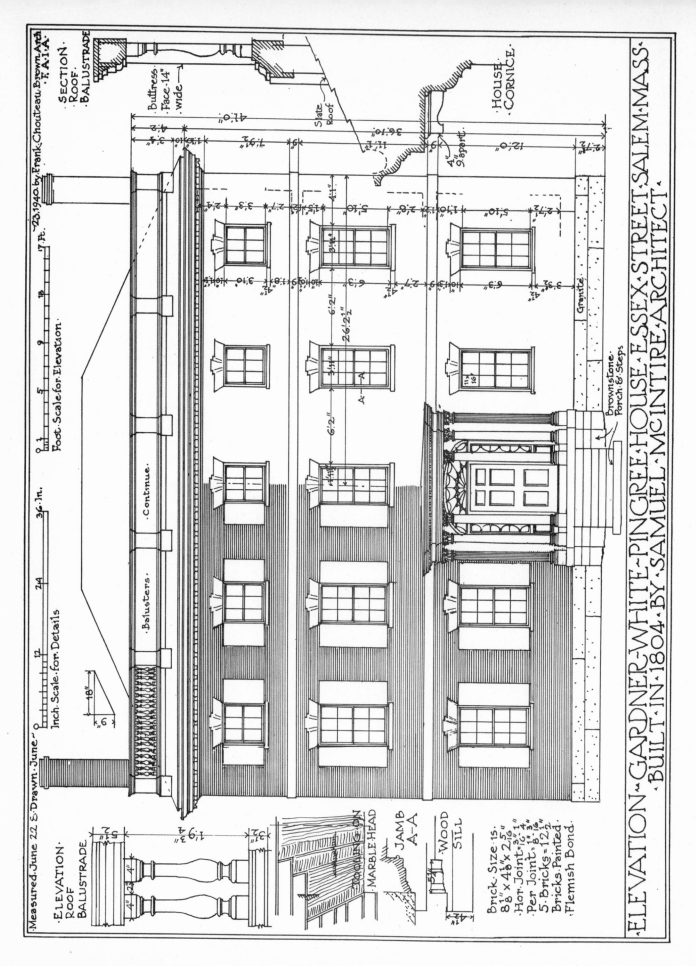

ELEVATION·GARDNER·WHITE·PINGREE·HOUSE·ESSEX·STREET·SALEM·MASS·
·BUILT·IN·1804·BY·SAMUEL·McINTIRE·ARCHITECT·

·SECTION·ROOF·BALUSTRADE·

Measured June 22 E. Drawn June 23.1940 by Frank Chouteau Brown, Arch. F.A.I.A.

Foot Scale for Elevation.

Inch Scale for Details

·ELEVATION·ROOF·BALUSTRADE·

·Balusters. ·Continue.

Buttress. Face 14" wide

Slate Roof

HOUSE CORNICE.

Granite

Brownstone. Porch & Steps

JAMB A-A

WOOD SILL

Brick Size 15.
8" x 4½" x 2½"
·Hor. Joint 3¼"
·Per Joint 1·3"
5 Bricks = 8½"
5 Bricks = 12.2"
·Bricks Painted
·Flemish Bond.

Front Drawing Room and Doorway to North Parlor, First Floor

Corner in Front Drawing
Room, First Floor

Entrance Hall and Stairway

DETAIL SHOWING TURN OF STAIR RAIL TO SECOND FLOOR

DETAIL OF NEWEL AND START OF STAIRS

CORNER OF HALL INSIDE ENTRANCE DOORWAY

General View of Dining Room, First Floor

Detail View of East Fireplace Wall, North Parlor, First Floor

VIEW INTO NORTH PARLOR
FROM FRONT DRAWING ROOM

East Wall of Southeast Bedroom, Third Floor

Corner in Southeast
Bedroom, Third Floor

Southwest Bedroom, Second Floor

East Fireplace Wall of Northeast Bedroom, Second Floor

Fireplace in Northeast
Bedroom, Second Floor

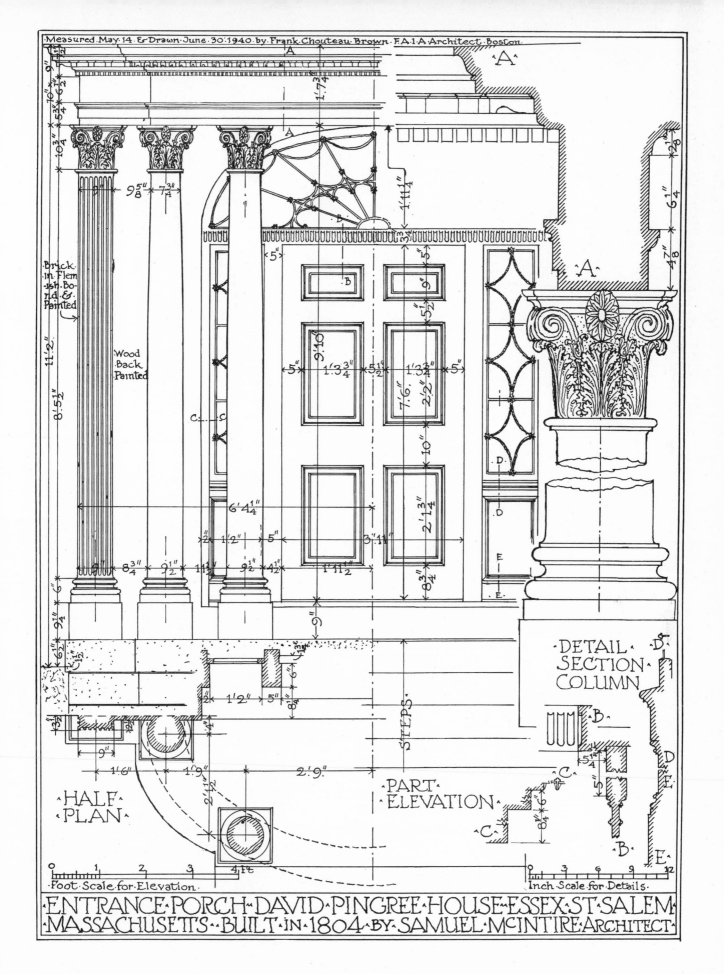

Measured May 14 & Drawn June 30 1940 by Frank Chouteau Brown F.A.I.A Architect Boston

Brick in Flemish Bond & Painted

Wood Back Painted

HALF PLAN

Foot Scale for Elevation

PART ELEVATION

STEPS

DETAIL SECTION COLUMN

Inch Scale for Details

ENTRANCE·PORCH·DAVID·PINGREE·HOUSE·ESSEX·ST·SALEM·
MASSACHUSETTS·BUILT·IN·1804·BY·SAMUEL·MCINTIRE·ARCHITECT

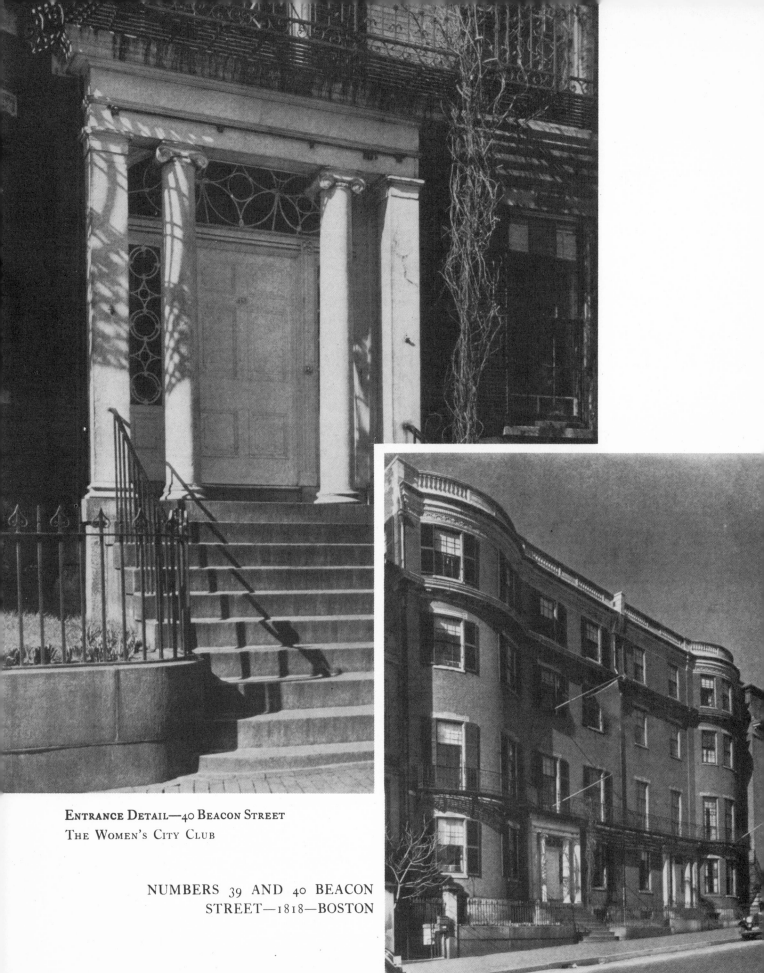

ENTRANCE DETAIL—40 BEACON STREET
THE WOMEN'S CITY CLUB

NUMBERS 39 AND 40 BEACON
STREET—1818—BOSTON

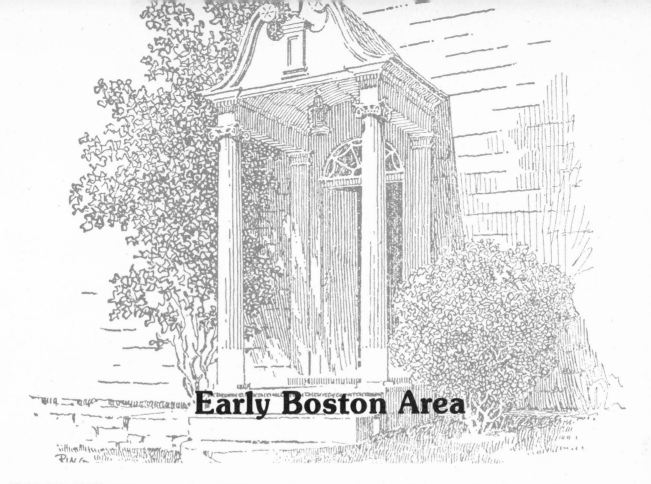

Early Boston Area

BUT it was not until March, 1628, that the newly formed Plymouth Company transferred to six men—Sir Henry Roswell, Sir John Young, Thomas Southcote, John Humfrey, John Endecott, and Simon Whitcomb—a strip of land defined as extending from three miles north of the Merrimack to three miles south of the Charles Rivers, and running westward from the Atlantic coast into seeming infinity.

To effect the colonization of this new World property "The Governor and Council of the Massachusetts Bay in New England" was organized, with John Winthrop as its governing head. This group was to become generally known as "The Massachusetts Bay Company"—although it was not until March 4 of the following year (1629) that a Charter was finally secured from Charles the First of England.

In June, 1628, the first group of authorized settlers was despatched, under Captain John Endecott, who had been appointed Governor of the Colony (but not of the "Company," whose officers and members then remained in England). Before the arrival of this chartered group, Mr. Roger Conant (who had gone to Cape Ann in 1624 to help establish a fishing station which was abandoned a year or two later), had removed, with at least three others, to Salem; where the Massachusetts Bay Company new colonization group found them upon its arrival in 1628, which has been regarded as the date of the official settlement at Naum-keag, or Salem, on Massachusetts Bay.

By 1630, the owners of the Company charter had decided to push their colonization—and a total of seventeen vessels went forward during that year, fourteen of which sailed before the first of June. The first of these, the "Lyon," left England in February and arrived in Salem in May. The "Mary & John," carrying the Rev. John White and families from Dorchester, England, left March 20 and arrived at Nantasket May 30. Thence, its passengers proceeded to Mattapan and finally settled at Dorchester, which was later to become a part of the city of Boston.

After the arrival of Winthrop and Saltonstall, at Charlestown (or "Charlton," as it was called), the water supply was found to be unhealthy. On the invitation of William Blaxton, who was then living on the western slope of Beacon Hill, they decided to move across the river, which they did September 17, 1630—the official date of the settlement of Boston.

After they were well settled on the Boston side of the Harbor, on October 18, 1630, the first quarterly meeting of the "Court of Assistants," or General Court, was held, as was provided in the Charter. At this meeting, Boston, Dorchester, and Watertown, together with Salem—the first towns to be established by the Massachusetts Bay Company in this newly settled area—were formally assigned those names.

But although the water supply was now ample (the source in Spring Lane is, indeed, still flowing, and cannot be stopped, into the cellars of office buildings

PORTICO ADDED 1789—PETER HARRISON, ARCHITECT
KINGS CHAPEL—1749—CORNER TREMONT AND
SCHOOL STREETS

ASHER BENJAMIN, ARCHITECT
CHARLES STREET, A. M. E. CHURCH—1807—
CORNER OF CHARLES AND MT. VERNON
STREETS—BEACON HILL

"The Old North"
CHRIST CHURCH—1723—SALEM STREET,
BOSTON, MASSACHUSETTS

"The Old South"
MEETING HOUSE—1729—WASHINGTON ST.,
BOSTON, MASSACHUSETTS

DETAIL OF BALCONY ON SOUTH ELEVATION

THE OLD STATE HOUSE—1713-1747—
HEAD OF STATE STREET,
BOSTON, MASSACHUSETTS

thereabout!), William Blaxton did not get along as well as might be wished with the narrow minds and strict laws of his new associates. So, in 1634, he agreed to transfer all his property, including his apple orchard and pasturage on the south of Beacon Hill, to the Puritans for £30, which was paid by an assessment made upon all the settlers. A considerable part of this common purchase is still open to the public, as "Boston Common!" So Mr. Blaxton packed his "Canonical Cote" and his library of over 200 bound volumes, and moved southward, to Attleborough Gore—then a part of Massachusetts, but later made part of Rhode Island.

Boston, with a thin causeway connecting it with the mainland to the west, began to crowd its restricted area with houses, wharves, taverns, and business offices, until it became the most thriving business community of the Commonwealth. Most of its business area lay to the east and south of the steep pitches of Trimount, or "Beacon Hill," with what is now "State Street" and "Washington Street" as its principal thoroughfares.

The first Church, with mud walls and a thatched roof, was located upon State Street in 1632. The Town House, at its westernmost end, the first structure being of wood, was built about 1657-9 where the "Old State House" now stands. Burned in 1711, it was rebuilt of brick in 1712. Again it was burned, in 1747, with all the Town records, and was again rebuilt in 1748. Since that time it has passed through many vicissitudes and changes, until the present interior can bear no possible resemblance to what it may have been at its beginnings—but the brick walls, at least, must remain much as they were constructed in 1712.

When Faneuil Hall was built in 1742, its eastern end was upon the Harbor's verge. Later, docks were built out into the water; and later still, in 1826, the granite Quincy Hall Market was constructed upon a filling extending far to the east of Faneuil Hall.

Beacon Hill—whence came the early name of "Treamont" or "Trimont"—had originally three peaks, the westernmost being known as "Copley's Hill" or Mt. Vernon Hill and the eastern one being called "Cotton" or Pemberton Hill. The central, and highest, was known as Beacon Hill, from the mast with a barrel beacon, erected by order of the General Court in March, 1635, and continued until destroyed by a storm in November, 1789. This highest peak was situated directly back of the State House, until it was cut down in 1811 to about half its former height. The

State House, designed by Charles Bulfinch and built in 1795, cost $135,000, and is 172 ft. front by 65 ft. deep, the dome being 155 feet high, just about level with the former natural summit of the Hill.

The original building has been twice enlarged—first having an extensive ell added at the rear and, more recently, submitting to the addition of extensive wings, upon both sides, of marble. Fortunately, since that time, the paint that had obscured the colonial red brick and white marble color scheme of the original design since 1825, has been removed, and the Bulfinch portion of the building may again be clearly visioned, lacking only the substantial depths formerly provided by its end elevations. The building is unique among the State capitols of the world in its simplicity and restraint of appearance, and also in the arrangement for support of the dome by placing its lower drum over a pedimented attic treatment of the façade.

Bulfinch laid out Park Street anew in 1803, and the first four houses were built at the lower end in 1804. Mr. Thomas Amory also built the pretentious brick mansion on the corner of Park and Beacon Streets in the same year, and it was known as "Amory's Folly." It was occupied by Mr. Christopher Gore, while Governor, in 1808-1809, and later owned by Mr. Otis until bought by Mr. George Tichnor in 1830. The porch originally had stairways to the street on both sides. The first bathroom was installed on Park Street in 1848, using Cochituate water.

Almost the first house built upon Beacon Hill was Thomas Hancock's pretentious stone Mansion (1735-7) facing the Training Field, or what is now Beacon Street. When built, it was considered as being quite "out of town," and was finally torn down in 1863. The western parts of the Hill were purchased in 1796 by Harrison Gray Otis and Jonathan Mason, representing the Mount Vernon Proprietors, and they started to develop and build brick houses on the newly laid out streets. Harrison Gray Otis had built his first house (141 Cambridge Street, now the home of the Society for the Preservation of New England Antiquities) in 1795. While a porch was shown upon the dwelling in pictures of 1830, it probably was built with only a brick arched entrance enclosing elliptical top and side lights. The present porch is in part a restoration. Otis' second residence was built at what is now 85 Mount Vernon Street (usually known as the Sears House) in 1800. In 1807 he built his third residence (numbered 45 Beacon Street). All are believed to have been by Bulfinch, who also probably designed the

DETAIL OF CUPOLA AND DORMERS

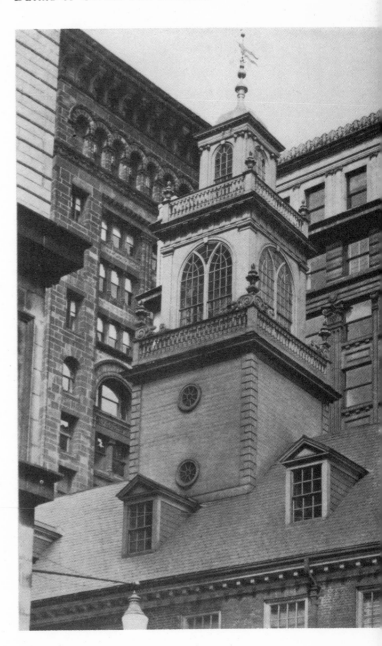

FANEUIL HALL (1742) ENLARGED BY CHARLES BULFINCH—1805-6—BOSTON, MASSACHUSETTS
Old bricks are 7⅛" x 3⅜" x 2" laid Flemish bond with ⅜" joint.
5 courses in 11¼ inches of height

SOUTH SIDE—FANEUIL HALL—1742—BOSTON, MASSACHUSETTS

Drawn April 3 1937 by Frank
Chouteau Brown A.I.A from
Measurements by James V. Dooley
& Charles H Smith 1936.

Marble, Belt
Course. 10″

Marble. 5′

N.B.
The Doorway &
Toplight & other
Detail suggested
within this Arch-
way is Conjectur-
al tho' based upon
old Photographs &
Fragments of Finish

Red
Brown
Brick of
8¼×4¼×2¼
5 Courses
equal 12½″
H & S=12½″
⅜″ Joint in
Flemish
Bond

App. Slope
Sidewalk

Brownstone Steps
& Slab

D

Iron Rail

HALF PLAN

Column
9″ Neck
& 10¾″
Base

Scale of Feet for Elevation.

Scale of Inches for Details.

ENTRANCE·PORCH·TICHNOR·HOUSE·BULFINCH·1804·
9·PARK·STREET·CORNER·BEACON·BOSTON··MASS'HTS.

122

THE BULFINCH BUILDING—1818—MASSACHUSETTS GENERAL HOSPITAL, FRUIT STREET
BOSTON, MASSACHUSETTS

QUINCY HALL MARKET—1826—EAST OF
FANEUIL HALL—1742—BOSTON, MASSACHUSETTS
ALEXANDER PARRIS, ARCHITECT

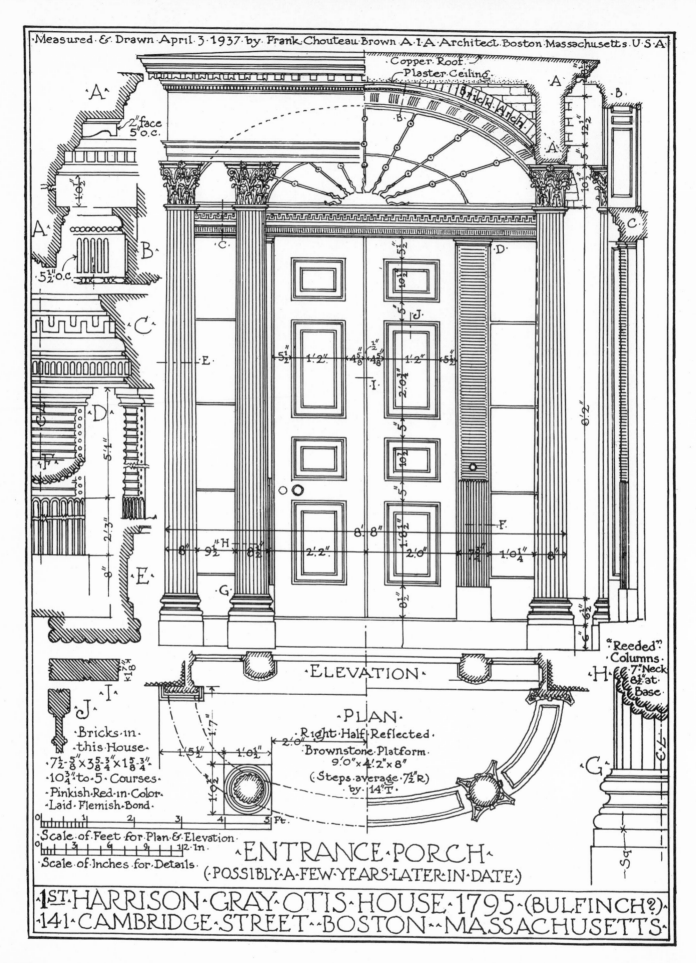

Measured & Drawn April 3 1937 by Frank Chouteau Brown A.I.A. Architect Boston Massachusetts U.S.A

Copper Roof
Plaster Ceiling
Brick Arch

· ELEVATION ·

· PLAN ·
· Right Half Reflected ·
· Brownstone Platform ·
9'0" × 4'2" × 8"
(· Steps average 7½"R)
by 14"T ·

"Reeded"
Columns
7" Neck
8½" at
Base

Bricks in
this House.
· 7½-⅝" × 3 5-3/8" × 1 5-3/4" ·
· 10¾ to 5 Courses ·
· Pinkish Red in Color ·
· Laid Flemish Bond ·

· Scale of Feet for Plan & Elevation ·
· Scale of Inches for Details ·

· ENTRANCE · PORCH ·
(· POSSIBLY · A · FEW · YEARS · LATER · IN · DATE ·)

·1ST· HARRISON · GRAY · OTIS · HOUSE · 1795 · (BULFINCH?)·
·141· CAMBRIDGE · STREET · BOSTON · MASSACHUSETTS·

124

FIRST HARRISON GRAY OTIS HOUSE—141 CAMBRIDGE STREET, BOSTON, MASS.

houses along Park Street, a great many more facing upon the principal streets of Beacon Hill, and many rows of dwellings in the lower part of the City, as well as the residential "Colonnade Row" along Tremont Street, now all supplanted by business buildings.

The house at 29A Chestnut Street, probably designed by Bulfinch, and at one time occupied by Edwin Booth, was the first house built by the Mount Vernon Proprietors. It dates from 1799 or 1800 and shows how most of these dwellings were first planned with the entrance upon the side of the house—in this case facing up the Hill. On the other hand, Nos. 55 and 57 Mount Vernon Street, built by Stephen Higginson, Jr., had their entrance doorways upon the western or down hill side, as still appears in the case of No. 55.

The three Chestnut Street houses, with delicately colonnaded entrances, numbered 13, 15, and 17, were built in 1806, also from Bulfinch's designs. They have behind them a row of three one-story brick stables— still to be seen on the south side of Mt. Vernon Street —along with the large arched passageway left for the crossing of the cattle from beyond to their pasturage rights on Boston Common. One of the paired houses at Nos. 39 and 40 Beacon Street, with fine marble entrances, built about 1818 (the upper story having been added about 1887), now the Women's City Club.

A number of the houses on Beacon Hill are built in pairs; and, occasionally, even in groups, or rows, of three or more. Architecturally, one of the most interesting of these is the pair at No. 54 and 55 Beacon

The Third Harrison Gray Otis House
THE WADSWORTH HOUSE—1807—45 BEACON STREET, BOSTON, MASSACHUSETTS
Charles Bulfinch, Architect

The Second Harrison Gray Otis House
THE SEARS HOUSE—C. 1800—85 MT. VERNON STREET, BOSTON, MASSACHUSETTS
Charles Bulfinch, Architect

CHARLES BULFINCH, ARCHITECT
NUMBERS 13, 15 AND 17 CHESTNUT
STREET—1806—BOSTON

Street, built about 1807, with three story wooden pilasters against their façades, and a particularly charming treatment of the first story with a colonnade of slight and delicately proportioned columns surmounted by a characteristic iron balcony of the period.

The exterior design of Bulfinch's own house (built 1799) may still be traced at 8 Bulfinch Street. Among his Boston public buildings, the Massachusetts General Hospital, off Fruit Street, was built in 1818; and one end of the huge structure of the India Wharf Stores may still be seen on India Wharf off Atlantic Avenue, although the extension of that Avenue in 1869 cut off more than half the length of the building, including its main central entrance feature. While a record of Boston architecture must make of Charles Bulfinch an important figure, it still gives no idea of the many imposing structures he designed that were built outside that city. Nor can it even suggest his many important city and community activities—such as being head of the Selectmen for many years, as well as performing important service as Street Commissioner at a time of large expansion of the city, so that he must have done much to complete and perfect Boston's present layout and City Plan.

BUILT IN 1807
Nos. 54 AND 55 BEACON STREET,
BOSTON, MASSACHUSETTS

OLD SENATE AND COUNCIL CHAMBER—"BULFINCH STATE HOUSE"—BEACON HILL

Beacon Hill, Boston

"BEACON HILL," in Boston, refers always to a somewhat undefined area, including a portion of the older and better residential district facing south toward the Common: while "Back of the Hill" has precisely the same connotation as is usually conveyed, in less altitudinous circles, by the equally descriptive phrase, "the other side of the railroad tracks." The entire Hill area is now bounded by the northern side of Boston Common—Beacon Street: its westernmost margin now ends at the Charles River Embankment, but in olden times Charles Street was as far as the land extended in that direction: Cambridge Street marks its northernmost —if less distinguished—limits; and where about the year 1800 its residential area extended as far east as Pemberton Square, or thereabouts,—it is now more strictly limited in that direction by Somerset Street.

In earlier, and some recent, numbers of this publication; something has already been written—as well as shown —both of the history and the structures within this limited area. It will now be attempted to give, somewhat more in detail, but nevertheless still an overmuch condensed record of, its history and development.

In the early history of this region, the fact that the Reverend William Blaxton (or Blackstone) was probably its original settler has been given, as well as something of his history after he turned over his orchard and farmstead—as well as his cow pasture (now Boston Common) to the too rigorous and closely crowding Puritans. His dwelling was probably located near the present intersection of Chestnut and Spruce Streets; while his orchard probably extended north easterly, up over the then wild and steeply rugged slopes of the Hill that protected his dwelling from the coldest winter storms, about where Mount Vernon, Pinckney, and Chestnut Streets now are, in the area immediately east of present Louisburg Square.

The old "Trimount," with its highest summit divided between three peaks, stood much as it had been in Blackstone's time very nearly up to 1790, at which time the original brick-stuccoed column from designs by Charles Bulfinch was erected upon the highest peak, with its base very nearly level with the top of the present State House pediment to mark the Beacon, that had occupied that position from 1635 until it was demolished by the November storm of 1789. The old Blaxton orchard still stood upon the western slope of the Hill; here and there an excavation had been made to obtain gravel; the western peak had been partly cut down to build-up Charles Street and extend the Hill's area to the West; a Reservoir was located near the top, and a Ropewalk or two had sprung up along the northern base of the slope, nearly parallel with the present Cambridge Street. An inclined gravity railroad, set up in 1803 to facilitate conveying the gravel of Mt. Vernon Hill down to the west, was called "the first railroad built in this country." In 1811 the highest summit of the Hill was reduced about sixty feet, to something approximating its present level, the old monument replaced by the present stone copy (the tip of which is just about the height of the old hill); and, about 1835, the third and easternmost peak, Cotton Hill, was finally leveled off.

Probably the earliest dwellings were built along the northern slope,—small wooden cottages for the families of workingmen, servants, and slaves. After the building of the new State House in 1795, fronting south upon the Common lands, Squire Otis and Sen. Mason tried, about 1802, to start a better class of residential building west of the State House. Before that time, only a half-dozen scattered dwellings were located upon the southern margin of this area, probably mostly wooden farmsteads,—with the single exception of the stone mansion of Thomas Hancock, built in 1737, and torn down in 1863. This was the first important dwelling facing on Beacon Street,—which then did not exist except as a rutted country lane. Later, at the time of the Revolution, there were probably standing at the east of the State House, three or four wood-

STAIRCASE IN GOVERNOR'S OFFICE—THE STATE HOUSE—BEACON HILL, BOSTON, MASSACHUSETTS

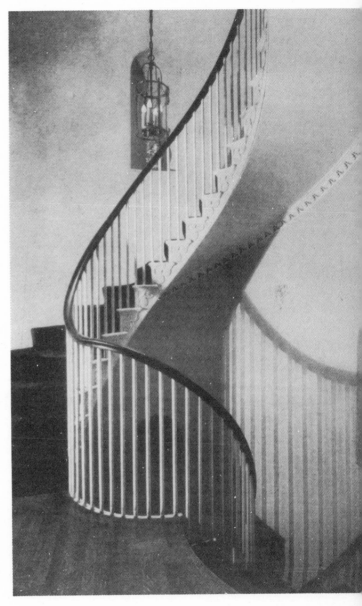

STAIRCASE—WOMEN'S CITY CLUB—1818—NO. 40 BEACON STREET, BEACON HILL, BOSTON, MASSACHUSETTS

STAIRCASE—OLD STATE HOUSE, BOSTON, MASSACHUSETTS

THE STATE HOUSE—1795—BEACON HILL, BOSTON, MASSACHUSETTS—CHARLES BULFINCH, ARCHITECT

en dwellings—and about as many to the west. Of these, the first was the Hancock Mansion, next beyond it were three wooden dwellings, belonging to the Copley family, the middle one being about on the site of the Somerset Club,—and the one furthest west dating possibly from as early as 1694. They all appear in an old water color view looking across the Common, painted in 1768.

This westernmost slope of "the Hill" was the property purchased by the "Mount Vernon Proprietors," organized probably in 1794 or 1795, and at first consisting of William Scollay, Charles Bulfinch, Jonathan Mason, Jr., Joseph Woodward, and Harrison Gray Otis. Of these, Messrs. Mason and Otis were the largest holders, and some of the others were shortly bought out by Benjamin Joy and Mrs. James Swan. The first of the new streets for this extensive real estate development were begun in 1799,—and it would appear that Mount Vernon Street—laid out along the natural ridge running nearly East and West, along with Chestnut Street—were the first planned to be built up,—and by 1805 and '06 a number of fine dwellings had been erected. It was at first the intention to develop the area in a semi-suburban manner,—with large houses, looking out over the slope to the Common, surrounded by ample yards, with stables at the north. (One of the latter, belonging to the Mason house, located at the head of Walnut Street is still to be seen placed back of the old house and now made into the dwelling numbered 24 Pinckney Street.) Just to the east of the Mason yard the two houses at Nos. 57 and 55 Mt. Vernon Street were built in 1804 with fronts and doorways looking west down the hill toward the water and across the driveway east of the Mason mansion, which was a wide three story brick house, built with central bay and pilasters in 1802, and torn down in 1836. The Thomas Bailey Aldrich dwelling (59 Mt. Vernon) was built, in 1839, over a portion of this driveway and yard, and the house and grounds extended to the west as far as No. 67. Other houses were built on the east up to Joy Street, as well as a number then being located along the east side of Charles Street,—which was then being graded—of which one, No. 85—built in 1809-10—still stands, with few exterior changes.

Meanwhile, the upper end of Chestnut Street was building up with "blocks," along with upper Mt. Vernon; which type of dwelling within the next score of years replaced most of the open yards along Mt. Vernon, Chestnut, and Beacon Streets. No. 87 Mt. Vernon (the Higgenson-Payne House) was built from Bulfinch designs in 1805; but most of the building on the Hill was arrested after 1807 by a business depression that set in about then begun or deepened by the Embargo placed upon U. S. Shipping at that time. The effect of a "depression" upon building in those days, seems hardly to have been distinguishable from that of a "recession" today!

Probably the grandest "Mansion" on the Hill was the house that Capt. Richard Crowninshield of Salem, built where the Theological School Chapel now stands on Chestnut Street. According to old legends it had a trick floor in the Dining Room through which the table could be made to disappear. Possibly this made the disposal of those gentlemen who might be peacefully reposing beneath it at the end of the evening all the easier and less conspicuous! It is a device that might even come in rather handy in these gate-crashing banquet days!

The block of three houses built by Mrs. Swan in 1806 for her daughters at 13-15-17 Chestnut fortunately still remains; and their stables are also clearly shown at the rear, on the South side of Mt. Vernon Street, on the back of the old Chestnut Street house lots. Although long since made over into Studios or Clubrooms, the wide openings through which the old carriages rolled out may still be traced,—along with the archway (although now closed) that formerly stood open, with stone paved ramp to the level beneath, up which the horses were brought from their stalls below for harnessing.

During the succeeding years, the lower western slopes of Beacon Hill were gradually being graded and redeemed from vacancy and wild pasturage, until by about 1825, this side of the Hill was also built-up down nearly as far as Louisburg Square on Mount Vernon Street, and on Beacon and Chestnut Streets houses had been built in as far west as Charles Street,—which had been filled and completed about 1805, along the margin of the basin flats. The last half-dozen houses on Beacon Street were destroyed by a fire that burned also the houses backing them on Chestnut; but fortunately did not affect the pair of dwellings built for James Colburn in 1807 at 54 and 55 Beacon Street. No. 58 was built the same year for Asher Benjamin, "housewright and architect"; and later, in 1833 and 34, he built the block of three houses on West Cedar Street between Acorn and Mt. Vernon, of which one, No. 9, was for his own occupancy.

It was not until 1834 that Louisburg Square was laid out, although it is recorded that it was not "adorned" (probably by the central enclosure of trees and fencing, along with the statues of Aristides and Columbus)

Central Door, Council Chamber to Hall
THE OLD STATE HOUSE—BOSTON, MASSACHUSETTS

Measured. Dec.18.1937 & Jan.8.1938 & Drawn. Jan.8.9.1938. at. Boston by·
Frank·Chouteau·Brown· Architect. A.1.A·

2'.0"
1'.0"

Roof. Slope. 1 to 2.
large. Welsh. slate.
& tinned. 4'.0" Back.

Roof·Balustrade·has·
disappeared·from·Nº·54.
& Dormers·altered.

Sash·up·this·Fourth·
Story·Nº·54·are·
12. Lts. D.H. and·in·
Nº·55. Casements.

Brick. are·
8½"x4"x2¼"
laid. in. ¼".
Close. joint·
in. Flemish·
Bond. &
painted. Buff·
Yellow.

19'.0"

2'.9" 3'.7"   6'.4"   3'.7" 2'.9"

· SECTION·
A – A

Sketch·
of·Bedmould·
Main·Ho·Cornice·

Sketch·
of·Cornice·First·
Story·Colonnade·

Approximate. Foot·
Scale. for. Sketches.

7" Dia·
Neck·

20. Flutes·
on. Column·

8" Dia·
Base·
·H·

· ELEVATION·

2'.11"   14'.11"   2'.8"   9'.6"
36'.0"

· PLAN·

11'.4"   7'.10"   7'.10"   1'.7"   10'.6"

These. Houses·
are. attributed·
to. Bulfinch·

DWELLING AT 55 BEACON STREET—1807—BEACON HILL, BOSTON

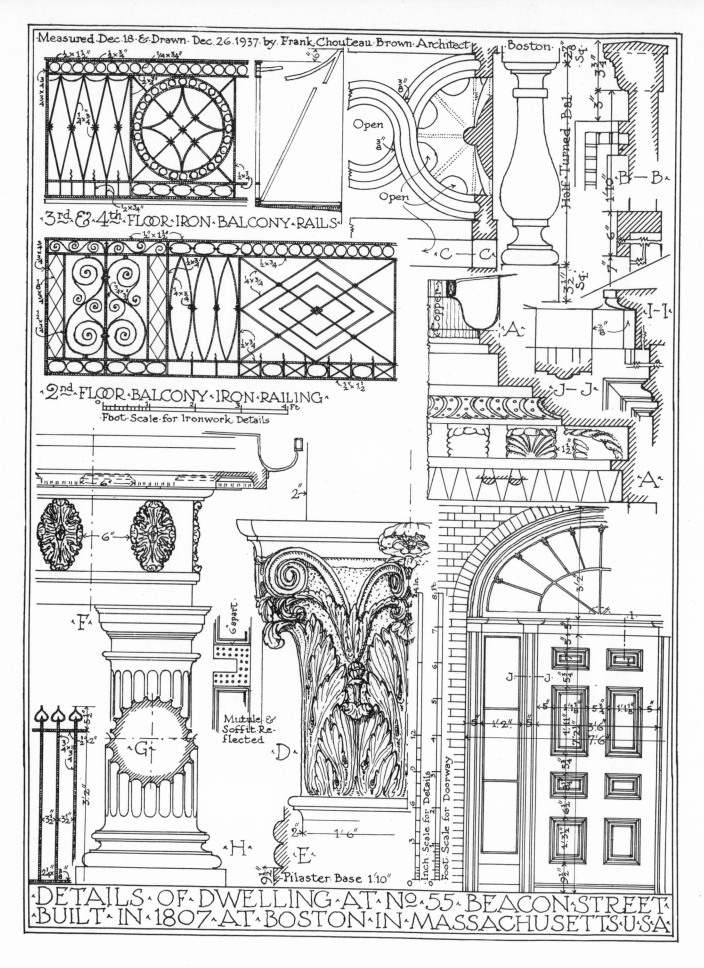

Measured. Dec.18 & Drawn. Dec.26.1937. by. Frank Chouteau Brown. Architect.

Boston.

3rd. & 4th. FLOOR. IRON. BALCONY. RAILS.

Open
Open

Half Turned Bal.

2nd. FLOOR. BALCONY. IRON. RAILING.

Foot Scale for Ironwork Details

Mutule & Soffit Reflected

6" apart.

Pilaster Base 1'10"

Inch Scale for Details
Foot Scale for Doorway

DETAILS. OF. DWELLING. AT. No. 55. BEACON. STREET.
BUILT. IN. 1807. AT. BOSTON. IN. MASSACHUSETTS. U.S.A.

until 1844,—by which time all of the front areas of the Hill had been pretty well built-up; as well as most of the narrower streets running down toward Cambridge Street upon its nether northern side. It was at about this same time that a few houses were built further west along Beacon Street, beyond Charles, of which the two shown at Nos. 73-75 are part of a granite block of six dwellings, most of which have since been considerably altered or enlarged.

A great many of the Hill houses have been altered on the interior, either to provide more comforts and

is visible of it, sandwiched between its two marble wings, with its Brobdingnagian rear extension to the north. On its interior, the three or four most important rooms have fortunately also been preserved,—including the domestic and charmingly detailed old Senate and Council Chamber; the bolder and more monumental old House (now used by the Senate) with its stone derived details carried out in wood, and the fine and dignified "Doric Hall" beneath it, with one or two old staircases.

While six of the historic older churches of Boston

INTERIOR OF ABOLITION CHURCH—(1806)—SMITH STREET, BOSTON, MASSACHUSETTS

advantages for their inhabitants—or to meet the changing styles and house fashions of later years. A very epidemic of marble mantels overflowed the elevation, for instance, while succeeding waves of decoration—of many styles and differing fashions—have elaborated the former chasteness of these earlier dwellings,—until, from all the flood, it sometimes seems that their Colonial detail had been entirely swept away—except the fine old staircases, the very craft of making which has in some cases also vanished.

The Hill's principal adornment still remains, of course, in the "Bulfinch State House,"—or what now

stand upon the very margins of the Hill, only one modest church structure was—so far as is known—ever built wholly within its sacrosanct area; and that —oddly enough—is the little Abolition Church, still to be seen in Smith Court, which was built in 1806 as an "African Baptist Church" with a school room upon the first floor,—in which was born, from the efforts of William Lloyd Garrison, the New England Anti-Slavery Society, in January of 1832. The building bears a marble tablet reading, "A Gift to Cato Gardiner, First Promoter of this Building, 1806." It is now occupied as a Synagogue.

Detail Doorhead—Governor's Office   Detail Doorhead—Council Chamber

THE STATE HOUSE—1795—BEACON HILL, BOSTON, MASSACHUSETTS

73-75 BEACON STREET—ABOUT 1844   55 MOUNT VERNON STREET—1804

DWELLINGS BEYOND CHARLES STREET AND WESTERN SLOPE OF BEACON HILL, BOSTON, MASSACHUSETTS

THE GOVERNOR CHRISTOPHER GORE HOUSE
1805-06—WATERTOWN, MASSACHUSETTS

Watertown, Massachusetts

HEN GOVERNOR WINTHROP arrived in Salem, Massachusetts, on June 12, 1630, Sir Richard Saltonstall was among his following. Not caring for the conditions they found existing in that Colony, shortly after their arrival, on June 17, Governor Winthrop and Sir Richard started out to find some better location in which they could settle,—and Winthrop tells in his Journal that "We went to Mattachusetts" (as Boston Harbor was known at that time) "to find out a place for our settleing down. We went up Mistick River about six miles. We lay at Mr. Mavericks and returned home Saturday." On July 1 he tells us that the "Mayflower" and "Whale" had arrived safe in Charlestown Harbor,—being followed by the "Talbot" on the 2nd, and the "Trial" upon the 5th—where John Endecott (to forestall an anticipated similar enterprise by Gorges men from the northern settlements) had previously made a small settlement and started the building of the "Great House" at Mishawan (Charlestown), to which the new settlers decided to come. And accordingly, at Charlestown were landed most of the passengers arriving on the four vessels named and the balance of the 1630 fleet.

As has been told elsewhere, they shortly thereafter removed from Charlestown to Boston, but meanwhile many of the large company—by some counts numbering nearly fifteen hundred souls—had gradually scattered and found themselves locations in the country

roundabout. Sir Richard Saltonstall, either at the time of his expedition of June 17, with Gov. Winthrop, or later, explored further up the Charles River, and was so impressed by the rich meadows found on tidal water, only five to six miles above the Harbor, that within forty-eight days after the arrival of the Arbella at Salem, or by August 1, 1630, he was organizing—along with thirty-nine others—a church at Watertown, which was the third to be set up in Puritan New England.

If Salem is to be regarded as the first settlement made (after Plymouth), upon Massachusetts Bay, and the Charlestown-Boston one the next in order,—then Watertown would become the third. It is true that Dorchester was settled in between, but the first group did not remain as a permanent settlement, and the place was resettled later with new arrivals, largely from Boston itself, with which Dorchester afterwards was joined. The large part of the original Dorchester group departed in 1636 to resettle in Windsor, Connecticut,—including almost the entire congregation of Rev. Philip Hooker; who was at the head of the second Church established in the Colony, the first having been set up at Salem.

No exact date for the settlement of Watertown has ever been established, and it is probable that the migration of the families of the forty signers was a gradual one from Boston to the Watertown meadows, probably none among the forty signers of the articles being then actually in residence upon the site. The Rev.

THE CALDWELL HOUSE—C. 1742—WATERTOWN, MASSACHUSETTS

George Phillips was the minister appointed to the Watertown congregation, which for fully twenty years remained the largest and most important of all the Massachusetts church organizations. On Sept. 17 (7th by old style), 1630, the "Court of Assistants," sitting in the "Great House" at Charlestown passed resolution "That Treamountain shall be Boston; Mattapan, Dorchester; and ye town up ye Charles River, Watertown."

On Nov. 30, 1630, the Court of Assistants assessed for the incomes of the two ministers then active; Mr. Wilson of Charlestown and Mr. Phillips in Watertown, upon the following basis;—a total of £ 60, divided equally between them, and imposed as follows,—£ 20 to Boston, £ 20 to Watertown, £ 10 to Charlestown, £ 6 to Roxbury, £ 3 to Medford, and £ 1 to Winnisimmet (Saugus & Revere). It would seem to be probable that this assessment was based upon an estimated proportionate balance among the churchmen in these several groups at that same time. In 1651 we were told by an early chronicler that Watertown had one hundred and sixty families, and that the town was largely agricultural in interest.

Watertown originally included Waltham, Weston, a large part of Lincoln, part of Sudbury, Wayland, part of Belmont, and Newtowne (Cambridge) east of Mount Auburn Cemetery; a large and rich agricultural area, and one still containing much rich architectural material, although most of the actual early buildings have disappeared because of the wealth,

prosperity, and business growth of the many important towns now within this same area, as well as the quickly acquired wealth of the prosperous owners of the old structures themselves.

The oldest house still standing within this area is the Abraham Browne house, in Watertown, near the further Waltham line. A few years ago this structure was on the verge of demolition, but it was preserved and restored by the Society for the Preservation of New England Antiquities. The earliest portion was built in 1663, as a "single" house, having one room on each of two floors, with an attic in a steep roof above. It so remained until about 1730, when an addition was placed upon the northern side of the original house, with double hung windows,—and the old casements on the north wall of the older portion were built into what then became an interior partition—and forgotten. Hence it was that, when the restoration was started, two original three-part casement frames were uncovered, the first that actually had been found in place up to that time in New England. They were badly rotted, and portions were missing, but of certain things there could be no doubt.

An accompanying sketch indicates this frame and some details of its construction. Of the head and sill pieces enough remained to make their sections and framing quite definite. The frame had no end jambs, using the upright studs for that purpose (F). The clapboards were nailed directly upon the upright studs, without exterior boarding. The intermediate mullions

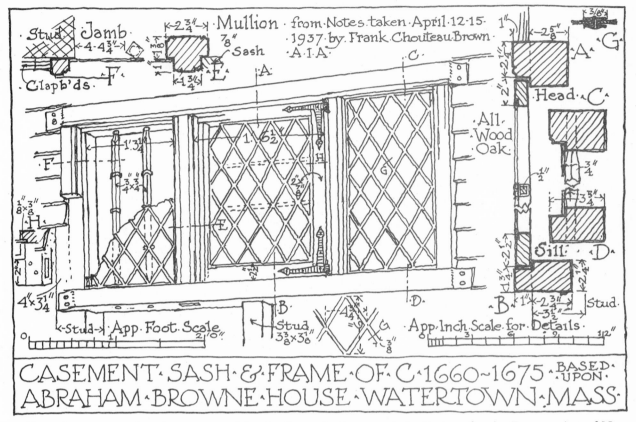

Stud. Jamb ·from·Notes·taken·April·12-15·
Mullion ·1937·by·Frank·Chouteau·Brown·
Sash ·A.I.A·
Clapb'ds Head·C·
All·Wood·Oak·
Sill·D·
App. Foot. Scale Stud·App·Inch·Scale·for·Details·

CASEMENT·SASH·&·FRAME·OF·C·1660~1675· BASED·UPON· ABRAHAM·BROWNE·HOUSE·WATERTOWN·MASS·

From fragments and sashes preserved by the Essex Institute and the Society for the Preservation of New England Antiquities, sash dimensions and "quarrel" (glass) sizes have been compiled. The lead "cames" are all of ⅜th inch face width, nearly flat, except where lined or grooved from pressure applied when being fitted tight against the glass along their edges.

Name of House	Location	Date	Outside size wood sash	Size Glass Quarrel
Aptucxet Trading Post	Bourne	1627	unknown	4½" x 5½" high
Deacon Browne House	Salem	1654	20" x 29"	3½" x 4" high
Abraham Browne House	Watertown	1663	18½" x 26½"	4¾" x 6" high
Perkins House	Lynnfield	1670-5	14½" x 28½"	5¼" x 6¼" high
Ward House	Salem	1684	19" x 30"	4¾" x 5¾" high
Forbes House	Bridgewater	?	18½" x 20"	5⅛" x 6¾" high

were clearly shown (E), but the molding along the lower edge of the head,—and the sides of the mullion —seems more like a shallow bead and fillet than the ogee used on the restoration. An upright stud coming in the middle of the space, framed into a notch in the back part of the crosspiece of the window frame on both top and bottom. The face treatment on the jamb was not found. It was evident it was narrow enough to allow the clapboards to stop against it and at the same time be nailed securely to the upright

stud. The holes to receive the upright stiffening rods for the fixed leaded lights, and the mortices for the mullions, were clearly given.

All this information has been assembled upon the accompanying sketch, along with some additional data as to sash and leading found in other locations. What dimensions it has been possible to assemble in regard to early casement sash sizes and glazing, have also been tabulated in the accompanying table. On the occasion of making replacement of the clapboards upon the

THE ARTEMAS WARD, JR., HOUSE
—1785—WESTON, MASSACHUSETTS

PORCH DETAIL

THE LAW OFFICE OF ARTEMAS WARD, JR.—1785—WESTON, MASSACHUSETTS

THE BENNETT HOUSE—C. 1780
—WAYLAND, MASS.

south side of the old house a couple of years ago, Mr. Sumner Appleton secured a photograph of the exterior of the wall, with the clapboards removed, showing the half-timber framework and the brick nogging, filled or "daubed" with clay, and "limed" or surface-washed to prevent washing away by what water might work through the protecting wood wall covering. In this connection it might be recalled that the name of this type of wall covering came from "clay-boards,"—so named because they were used to cover "clay walls" of houses. The manufacture and shipment of these clapboards back to England was a considerable business in New England from very early times. They were gotten out usually to 4′ 0″ lengths, ½″ thick on the heavier edge, and thinned to ⅛″ upon the other. They were six to eight inches wide, and the ends were beveled to lap over when laid. The best white pine was used and considerable skill was required to "rive out" the clapboards with the "frow" at the least lumber waste. The first mention of this product in New England was in Gov. Winthrop's Journal, "Mr. Oldham had a small house near the weir at Watertown, made all of clapboards, burned August, 1632."

This summarizes most of the definite information known of early wooden casement windows in eastern Massachusetts. They were used in houses built as late as 1720 or 25, in the large coastal towns or cities,— and probably for another ten or twenty years in the more remote inland communities; while the newer Georgian double hung sash were gradually coming into use in different localities beginning about 1705 or 1710 and continuing over later years.

To pass from the Seventeenth Century Browne House to the later primness of the Governor Gore place is a matter only of a mile or more, and nearly a hundred and fifty years; but it is possible to find many examples representative of the years between, without going outside the confines of old Watertown,—or, indeed, without straying far from the next few miles of the old Highway, laid out along the trail of the earliest Indian travel, in what was long known as the "Connecticut Path," which passes only a hundred rods or so in front of the Governor's Mansion.

You can follow the road from Waltham to Watertown, from there through Kendall Green and Weston, and so on to Wayland, and—if you wish to visit the old Wayside Inn—over the old four arch bridge, 1791, into Sudbury,—or branch off on the Connecticut Path toward Hartford. Shortly after passing through Weston Center, the road passes—on its left—the Golden Ball Tavern, 1768, and on its right, the Artemas

THE GOLDEN BALL TAVERN—1753—CENTRAL AVENUE, WESTON, MASSACHUSETTS

THE BIGELOW HOUSE, WESTON, MASSACHUSETTS

Ward Jr. House, 1785; and his picturesque little Lawyers Office, built about 1785, almost across the way, nestling under an umbrageous and historic elm.

Legend has it that this charming little "houselet" was built for a firm of lawyers, who, after a few years practice together, agreed to disagree—and parted. One kept to the old office, while his partner signed a paper undertaking not to open any competitive establishment within the same township. This he did, maintaining strictly to the letter of his bond,—and so one finds another little lawyer's office, dating from nearly 1800, a scant couple of miles further along the "Path," being perhaps as far as ten to fifteen feet over the line into the adjoining township of Wayland. It would seem that lawyers were—well, shall we say, lawyers;—even in those dear departed days!

For other examples covering these intervening periods, Waltham itself still preserves, one on each side of this very same roadway, and just before reaching the Browne house, a small gambrel cottage known as the Caldwell House, and the uncompromising squareness of the old Bemis homestead, across the road.

The Governor Christopher Gore place, 1805-6, on the border marches between Waltham and Watertown, has been rescued recently from a double score of years of gradual disintegration, both moral and physical. Some twenty-five or so years ago, it was willed to the Episcopal Diocese of Boston, to be the site of a long-projected Episcopal Cathedral. After more years of anxious waiting, it was sold, and passed by turns rapidly through the hands of real estate agents, legal officials and factors; became the "office building" of an automobile manufactory, and an airplane plant; was a Country Club and a Golf House,—and just as it was about to be demolished to turn the Deer Park into more remunerative small house lots, its plight was recognized, and a few energetic individuals and Societies banded themselves together to preserve the house and what remained of its former dependencies.

Unfortunately, since one Saturday a quarter-century ago, when the Boston Architectural Club made the unusual old dwelling and its grounds an excuse for a summer outing, or "Field Day" (the occasion—by the way—on which the principal early set of pictures of the house was taken) many changes have been made by transitory and passing tenants. The old balustrade about the roof has fallen, or been removed—as has also the gray and white paint that was lying in many coats over its old walls of small and pink brick, laid closely in Flemish fashion. The old garden and brick

THE BEMIS HOUSE—
1740—WALTHAM, MASS.

THE HAGAR HOUSE, WESTON, MASSACHUSETTS

NORTH ELEVATION THE GOVERNOR CHRISTOPHER GORE
HOUSE—1805-06—WATERTOWN, MASSACHUSETTS

Courtesy Historic American Building Survey

SOUTH ELEVATION

DETAIL OF SOUTH ELEVATION (1912)   DETAIL OF SOUTH ELEVATION (1937)

greenhouses have been obliterated; quaint coal grates; silver hardware and bronze fixtures, with crystal chandeliers, have vanished,—along with truly mediaeval hooded tubs and curious early plumbing equipment, the silk velour curtains, dashing sleighs, and the "orange-colored coach," in which, gay with flashing harness and liveried coachmen, footmen and outriders, the Governor used to make his imposing progress, from Mansion to State House, and then home again!

The type of so-called "Southern plan,"—with lower wings and end pavilions supporting each side of the central two story mansion—has only a few counterparts in New England; two in eastern Rhode Island, at Poppasquash and Portsmouth,—and at least one other in Massachusetts. In the case of Gore Place, this Southern expansiveness of plan is accompanied by a most incongruous, if characteristically New England, paucity and reticence of detail, which, now the eaves balustrades are lacking, establishes an almost Puritanical rigor and baldness of aspect.

Yet, despite the ravishment of its parts, accessories, and furnishings; the substitution of some heavy later mantels for more delicate originals, Gore Place well repays a visit by its fine flavor of a vanished graciousness of living,—such as is delicately expressed in the pure and flowing lines and fine sweep of the curving stairway—that can have had only too few enduring expositions in the grim business of living according to the dictates of religion and a Puritan conscience, in old time New England!

THE ABRAHAM BROWNE HOUSE—1663—562 MAIN STREET, WATERTOWN, MASSACHUSETTS
Room on First Floor

Photograph made in 1934, before restoration

This house illustrates the essentially English half-timber construction of the architecture of the early Colonies

THE ABRAHAM BROWNE HOUSE
—1663—562 MAIN STREET,
WATERTOWN, MASSACHUSETTS

VASSALL-CRAIGIE-LONGFELLOW HOUSE—1759
105 Brattle Street, Cambridge, Massachusetts

Cambridge, Massachusetts, Part I

THE present City of Cambridge had its origin when a part of the area between Charlestown and Watertown was selected as a "fit place for a fortified town" in December of 1630, by the colonists then settling at Boston and Charlestown. It was also agreed that the officers and assistants would all build dwellings there during the following year. But by the end of 1631 only Dep. Gov. Thomas Dudley and Simon Bradstreet had actually built; and Gov. Dudley had his home taken down and re-erected in Boston.

Nevertheless, on February 3, 1631-32, the Governor and assistants ordered "that there should be three scoore pounds levyed out of the several plantations within the lymitts of this pattent toward the makeing of a pallysadoe aboute the newe towne,"—and it was as "Newe Towne" that Cambridge was known until May 2, 1638, when the change of name was authorized. This levy was distributed as follows: "Watertown, viii £.; the Newe Towne, iii £.; Charlton, vii £.; Meadford, iii £.; Saugus & Marble Harbor, vi £.; Salem, iv £. x s.; Boston viii £.; Rocksbury, vii £.; Dorchester, vii £.; Wessagusset, v £.; Winettsemet, xxx s." The enclosure was actually constructed, and surrounded by a "fosse," or ditch, beginning at "Wind Mill Hill" (now end of Ash St.) and continuing along the north side of the present Common, and then onwards to the river.

As the space between the two earlier settled towns appeared very limited to the new settlers, especially when the congregation of Thomas Hooker began to arrive, its area was enlarged in 1634 to include Brookline (Muddy River),—which was lost again when Mr. Hooker and his followers left for Hartford a few years later! Then Brighton and Newtown, across the river, Arlington (Menotomy) and most of what is now Lexington were added to the Cambridge area. Still later more land was taken from Billerica (Shawshine), parts of Bedford and Carlisle, and Tewksbury and Chelmsford.

In 1664 Newton established its own church, being finally separated in 1688. "The Farms" (Lexington) had secured its church in 1696, and was incorporated in 1713. Part of Watertown was annexed in 1754 and 1755, and, in 1802, part of Charlestown, now known as Somerville.

The growth of New Towne was very rapid. On March 29, 1631, forty-two people were listed as inhabitants, although these may have been only the names of the then established lot owners. One of the earliest references to any sort of building law in the New Colonies is in a letter of Thomas Dudley's, in which he says "we have ordered that no man there shall build his chimney with wood nor cover his house with thatch." If this order was obeyed, these new structures were being built upon the most permanent basis then employed—which would be easily possible if their owners were living in Boston or Charlestown, and could row back and forth while the new buildings

GENERAL WILLIAM BRATTLE HOUSE—1727
42 BRATTLE STREET, CAMBRIDGE, MASSACHUSETTS

across the River were being constructed.

There was a ferry at about the present location of Brighton bridge; while a bridge and causeway across the marshes to the Ferry landing was being planned at the south end of the present Dunster St. as early as December 7, 1635. But before that, in 1631, a canal was cut from the channel in the Charles River through the marshes to firm land near the center of the Town settlement. It was 12 feet broad and 7 feet deep, and cost 30 £. This indicates the early importance of transportation by waterway in American settlements. Indeed, the entire Cambridge side of the river was marshy and low. The only embankment remaining from the fortifications built by the besieging American army during the Revolution, now preserved as a small park in Cambridge, was originally erected upon a knoll then surrounded by marshland.

At this early date, the river and marsh were part of a larger tidal basin that included the Cambridge and Charlestown banks, and, on the south, beyond Beacon Hill, water and marsh extended way across to Washington Street and as far west as the highlands of Roxbury. It further continued along the Brookline (then Muddy) River and the Newton banks of the Charles as well.

The two first ministers in Boston and Cambridge were Mr. Cotton and Mr. Hooker. They were upon opposite sides in the then highly important Antinomian and Famalistic controversies. Matters came to such a pass that, in 1635 and 1636, most of the First

APTHORP HOUSE—1761, NO. 15 PLYMPTON STREET, CAMBRIDGE, MASSACHUSETTS

APTHORP HOUSE—Detail of Mantel in Dining Room

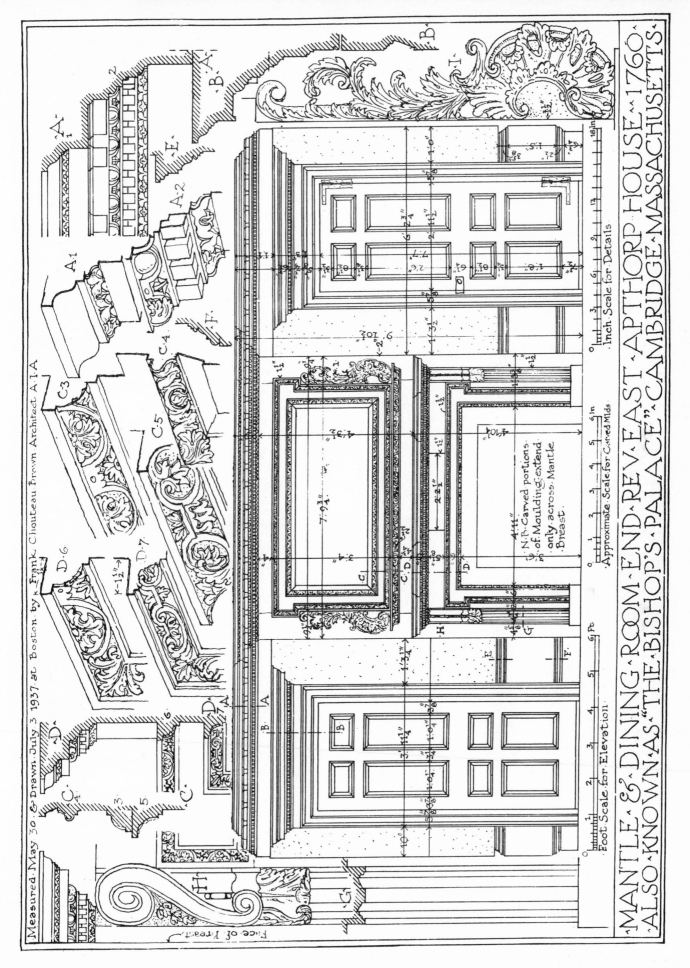

MANTLE & DINING ROOM END REV EAST APTHORP HOUSE 1760
ALSO KNOWN AS "THE BISHOP'S PALACE" CAMBRIDGE MASSACHUSETTS

Measured May 30 & Drawn July 3 1937 at Boston by Frank Chouteau Brown Architect A.I.A

N.B. Carved portions
of Moulding extend
only across Mantle
Breast.

Face of Breast

THE JAMES READ HOUSE—1725, NO. 55 BRATTLE STREET, CAMBRIDGE, MASSACHUSETTS

DETAIL OF DOORWAY

Church congregation from Cambridge removed with their minister, Mr. Hooker, to Hartford, Connecticut. This exodus took away more than fifty families, and lost the town of Brookline to Cambridge, as it had been given only if Thomas Hooker and his following should remain! In fact, much of the continuous plea for more land during these first years was perhaps as much as anything to provide an excuse for the removal of this group. Though, if we allow for the large amount of swampland, and the already established limits of Charlestown (then including Somerville and East Cambridge) and Watertown (which then came to the nearer line of Mt. Auburn Cemetery) there was not much usable land remaining, especially for the grazing of large herds of cattle and sheep that belonged to these first settlers, mostly concerned with farming.

Cambridge was adopted as the site of the new college on November 15, 1637, which was then ordered to be established at Newtowne, and 2⅔ acres were set apart for that purpose, including the present sites of Holworthy, Stoughton, and Hollis Halls. On March 13, 1638-9 it was named after John Harvard, who had in his will left the new College half his estate, £ 7000, and all his library—260 volumes.

Oldest among present Cambridge dwellings is the Cooper-Austin House, on Linnaean Street, which is owned by the Society for the Preservation of New England Antiquities and was built by Deacon John Cooper, in 1657. In evidence, was his license from the town, given in that year "to fell timber on the Cow Common for his building." At that time, and for many years after, the "Cow Common" extended northward to this location. Linnaean Street, then "Love Lane," was laid out in 1725. Beams and frame are of hewn oak, the timbered ceiling in the "East Parlor" being one of the finest in the vicinity.

John Cooper was a selectman, town clerk, and deacon. In an inventory of the estate, taken in 1783, the house was valued at £ 100, and 11½ acres of land at £ 345. In 1807 the house passed into the Austin family, and repairs made at that time may have included the first story entrance vestibule. About 1820 a fire damaged the west side, and the earliest remaining room and fireplace is now at the right of the entrance.

Until within a few years, Cambridge has been fortunate in that its business district developed largely in the portions nearer Boston and the River; so that the part lying beyond Harvard Square, out as far as Mount Auburn Cemetery, has remained a residential district, affected only by the expansion of the University. Consequently, there may still be seen, within less than a mile along Brattle Street, many imposing old dwellings that were known, before the Revolution, as "Tory Row." So by ignoring intervening houses of more recent date, in the progress of a short walk one may see more important old houses—important both architecturally as well as historically or from association with famous owners or occupants—than anywhere else so near a large city in all New England.

But first, we should notice two historic dwellings near Harvard Square. On Harvard Square is Wadsworth House, built for President Benjamin Wadsworth, in 1726, and used as the official dwelling of the Presidents of the College for over a hundred years. It is still maintained for College purposes; and its main outlines—of roof gambrel, dormers, windows, and porches—have been carefully preserved. It was occupied for a short time as Washington's headquarters, before his removal to the larger Longfellow House.

Another old building in this near vicinity is Apthorp House, sometimes known as "The Bishop's Palace," which was built in 1761 by the Rev. East Apthorp, the first rector of Christ Church, when he married Elizabeth, niece of Gov. Hutchinson and granddaughter of Gov. Shirley. Following his graduation from Jesus College, Oxford, in 1759, he (a native of Boston) was appointed missionary to Cambridge and returned here by the Society for the Propagation of the Gospel in Foreign Parts. One of his sisters married Thomas Bulfinch, and was the mother of Charles Bulfinch.

The Rev. Apthorp's father, a wealthy merchant and pillar of King's Chapel, was also Commissary and Paymaster of the British forces in Boston. This background of wealth, education, and travel fully explains the outstanding elegance of the house he built, which remains conspicuous, even today.

The Rev. East Apthorp gave up his Cambridge ministry and went to England in 1764, his house being sold, in 1765, to John Borland, husband of Anna Vassall, for one thousand pounds. When Borland was forced to leave Cambridge, as a well known Tory, the property was confiscated and used by the Committee of Safety during the Revolution, at one time quartering three companies of troops. After Burgoyne's surrender at Saratoga, General William Heath wrote General Washington, "Gen. Burgoyne is in Mr. Borland's house, formerly Putnam's quarters, and the other principal officers in the town of Cambridge."

In 1784 the house was purchased by Jonathan Simpson, Jr., husband of Jane Borland, who repaired and

JUDGE JOSEPH LEE-NICHOLS HOUSE—
159 BRATTLE STREET, CAMBRIDGE

BUILT ABOUT 1660—REMODELED ABOUT 1760

165

occupied it, and at this time the upper story may have been added. Although, according to tradition, it was built for the slaves of John Borland, the rooms now are paneled in a style that would hardly justify that use—unless the slaves were lodged in the low upper attic, above the third floor. During this occupancy, both Linden and Plympton streets were laid out through the property to meet the real estate boom caused by the opening of the "new bridge" in 1793. Capt. Thomas Warland came into possession in 1803, and it remained in that family until 1897, when Randolph Hall, a college dormitory, was built on Bow Street, within the old box garden, a small part of which remains in the courtyard between the two buildings.

The Brattle House, on Brattle Street, formerly had in its grounds to the east, the old "Town Spring," which led into a pond, which had been parked and beautified until it was known as one of the show places of New England. The present dwelling was built by Gen. William Brattle, about 1727. It still retains a few of the paneled rooms, and a fine stairway with hand carved balusters. The porch is—as usual—a later addition. Gen. Brattle was one of the richest men in Cambridge, and Major-general of all the province from 1771, an overseer at Harvard, and a well known Tory. The house was occupied by Major Thomas Mifflin, first *aide-de-camp* to General Washington, and Commissary-general during the siege of Boston.

Nearby, across the street from the Brattle House, is the Read House, probably built by James Read, who came from Kent, England, in 1725. In the southwest chamber is an inscription, traced on the wet plaster, which reads, "James Read, May 18, 1738." This house has been many times changed, but

EAST PARLOR FIREPLACE, COOPER-AUSTIN HOUSE

COOPER-AUSTIN HOUSE—1657
21 Linnaean Street, Cambridge, Massachusetts

"ELMWOOD"—1760—CORNER OF MT. AUBURN STREET AND
ELMWOOD AVENUE, CAMBRIDGE, MASSACHUSETTS

MANTEL, SOUTHWEST ROOM, FIRST FLOOR

the garden between it and Brattle Street has been maintained now for many years, and certainly since 1866. The simple but unusual details of the entrance doorway are now upon the face of a vestibule, to which it was probably advanced from the main wall of the house at the time the vestibule was added.

Farther along on Brattle Street and facing Long-fellow Park is the well known Vassall-Craigie-Long-fellow House, the Mecca of all visitors to Cambridge.

Built by Col. John Vassall, in 1759, this house was General Washington's headquarters in 1775. It was lived in by Dr. Andrew Craigie, 1793-1819, and he made additions to the house at the back. After Mrs. Craigie's death, in 1841, Henry Wadsworth Long-fellow, who had occupied rooms in the house from 1837, in Mrs. Craigie's lifetime, became the owner in 1843. He died in 1882, and the estate continues in the possession of his descendants. Large and stately, with certain Victorian changes and its literary flavor, this house is one of the best specimens of Colonial architecture in Cambridge.

Half a mile beyond, at the corner of Kennedy Avenue, stands the Judge Joseph Lee-Nichols House, beautifully preserved and maintained by its present architect-owner. The house dates from about 1660, although the third story was probably a later addition. The rooms on either side of the front hall are twenty feet square.

Elmwood Avenue, leading off Brattle Street to the left, brings us to "Elmwood"—where lived for many years James Russell Lowell, the scholar and poet. In 1848, he thus described his first study at Elmwood: "Here I am in my garret. I slept here when I was a curly-headed boy, and in it I used to be shut up without a lamp—my mother saying none of her children should be afraid of the dark. It is a pleasant room facing—almost equally—towards the morning and the afternoon sun. In winter I can see the sunset, in summer I can see it only as it lights up the tall trunks of the English elms in front of the house, making them sometimes, when the sky behind them is lead-covered, seem of the most brilliant yellow. In winter, my view is a wide one, taking in a part of Boston. As the spring advances and one after the other of our trees puts forth, the landscape is cut off from me, piece by piece, till, by the end of May, I am closeted in a cool and rustic privacy of leaves. Then I begin to bud with the season, when I can sit at my open window and my friendly leaves hold their hands before my eyes to prevent their wandering to the landscape. I can sit down and write."

DETAIL OF PORCH

WADSWORTH HOUSE—1726—
HARVARD SQUARE,
CAMBRIDGE, MASSACHUSETTS

Measured March 17 & Drawn 29 & 30 1933   by Frank Chouteau Brown Architect AIA

·A· Cornice

·B· Cap·

Turned

·C· Base·

·D· Pedestal·

Old Blind

Old Blind Detail

Clapboard

Soffit

Col.

·ELEVATION·

·PLAN·

Foot Scale for Drawing

Inch Scale for Details

(Partly Reflected)

Door 1½" th

·ENTRANCE·PORCH·&·DOORWAY·WADSWORTH·HOUSE·
·1726·HARVARD·SQUARE·CAMBRIDGE·MASSACHUSETTS·

CHRIST CHURCH—1761—GARDEN STREET, CAMBRIDGE, MASSACHUSETTS

GENERAL VIEW FROM EAST, ACROSS OLD BURIAL GROUND

Cambridge, Massachusetts, Part II

STARTING, as the settlement did, without formality; Cambridge — rather like Topsy—"just growed." And the rapidity of its growth was somewhat determined by its location between such early and important settlements as Charlestown and Watertown.

One of the earliest thoroughfares in the Colony was the pathway connecting these two early townships. As we have seen, Watertown was set up by men living in Boston and Charlestown. They were able to construct their new dwellings in less haste, as they were already fairly well housed, but were removing to more open country so they might increase their livestock and take up farming more exclusively. Consequently, there must have been an unusual amount of travel along the northern bank of the Charles. Any Boston dweller would most easily ferry across the River, below the marshes, and then take the Charlestown road, cutting inland almost in a direct line to Watertown Square (as it is today), thus leaving all the marshland on the Cambridge bank of the river to his left. This pathway came later to be known as "the King's Highway."

Leaving Charlestown, this road entered Cambridge over what is now Kirkland Street, crossed the Common near the Washington Elm, then through Mason and Brattle Streets and Elmwood Avenue, where it passed the end of the lane leading down to the ferry to Brighton, and continued on to Watertown, Waltham, and across the river to Newtown. The first settlement of Cambridge was made between this roadway and the river, to the south of the Common, in the area now covered by the new College "Houses" of the University,—or, at least, so much of it as was then above water—and between the Charlestown and Watertown boundaries, which were less than a mile apart.

Of especial interest to architects should be the record of the "first house built in Cambridge," as well as a word about its first owner. As early as March 10, 1628-29, the Massachusetts Bay Company in England agreed with one Thomas Graves, an "engineer" of Gravesend, to go to New England and lay out the town of Charlestown. Graves arrived in Salem, early in July, 1629, with Higginson. He went at once to Charlestown, laid out its plan, and directed the building of the palisade, and its "Great House." As part of his agreed recompense he was given one hundred acres of land, located in what is now East Cambridge but was then Charlestown; for, on March 6, 1632, we find, in the record fixing the boundaries between Charlestown and Cambridge, the agreement that "all the lands impaled by Newe Towne men, with the necke thereunto adjoyneing whereon Mr. Graves dwelleth, shall belong to said New Towne." Mayhap it was this same Thomas Graves who laid out the town of Woburn in 1640, but at any rate he sold his house in October, 1635, to Mr. Atherton Haugh, and in August, 1706, it was transferred to Spencer Phips, and belonged to Lt.-Gov. Phips when he died in his mansion, the

JOHN HICKS HOUSE—
1762—BOYLSTON
AND SOUTH STREETS,
CAMBRIDGE, MASS.

Winthrop Place, on Arrow Street, near Bow, in 1757.

But the major part of the Cambridge houses were grouped south of Harvard Square to the River, the first—which burned in 1666—being started by Thomas Dudley, on what is now Dunster Street, early in 1631.

The dwelling of Thomas Hooker, as well as of his succeeding ministers, stood where Boylston Hall now is,—and the house of the first President of Harvard, Henry Dunster, as well as the place where Stephen Daye's printing press was first set up, stood about where Massachusetts Hall stands.

Away from Tory Row and its environs, the old Hicks house is now located at the corner of Boylston and South Streets. It was built in 1760 at the corner of Dunster and Winthrop Streets by John Hicks, a master carpenter, for his own home. He was born in 1725, and participated in the Boston Tea Party, but was killed while fighting the retreating British from Lexington, on April 19, 1775. After his death, the building was used by General Putnam as an office. Previous to 1850, the John Vassall house was the only one on that side of Brattle Street for almost three-quarters of a mile, from Ash Street to Elmwood. A part of the western end of this house was probably built in 1636, by William Adams, on a site that was then outside the palisade. In 1682 it came into the possession of Capt. Andrew Belcher, whose son inherited the house in 1717 and married the daughter of Lt.-Gov. Partridge of New Hampshire. He later served 27 years as Royal Governor of Massachusetts,

New Hampshire, and New Jersey. John Vassall came into possession in 1736. He had married Elizabeth, daughter of Lt.-Gov. Spencer Phips, in 1734. His son, Maj. John, Jr., who built the Vassall-Craigie-Longfellow house in 1759, was born here, as well as a daughter, Elizabeth, who married Thomas Oliver, who built "Elmwood."

Col. Henry Vassall, a brother of John, Sr., took over the property in 1741, and shortly after married Penelope Royall, of Medford, and enlarged the house for her upon its eastern side five years later in 1746.

"The Marble Chamber," in this newer portion, was so called in a sworn inventory of Henry Vassall's estate, dated 8 Sept. 1769.

His widow, Mrs. Vassall, removed to Antigua, leaving her "medicine chest," at the request of the Provincial Congress. Only one other such chest, at Roxbury, was then available to the newly formed American army, and Vassall House became the medical headquarters under Dr. Church, who with Dr.

Foster, lived and ran the army hospital there.

The plan is unusual, with two separate halls and staircases, to west and east, the space between—originally open, with a bay toward the river—having been comparatively recently filled in by a central room, with a beam supported by Doric columns. In 1841 a fire damaged the eastern part of the house, burning the roof and five dormers then on that side.

Thomas Oliver built "Elmwood" shortly after his marriage to Elizabeth Vassall, granddaughter of Lt.-Gov. Phips, in 1760, and just after the land had been transferred from Watertown to Cambridge, in 1754. His maternal grandmother, Mrs. James Brown of Antigua, married Isaac Royall of Medford as her second husband. Oliver became Lieutenant Governor in 1774, just in time to be mobbed by the populace on September 2 of that year. The house was used as a hospital during the British occupation of Boston. "Elmwood" was later occupied by Elbridge Gerry of Marblehead, a signer of the Declaration of Independ-

MANTEL AND END, SOUTH EAST ROOM, FIRST FLOOR
"ELMWOOD"—1760—CORNER MT. AUBURN ST. AND ELMWOOD AVE., CAMBRIDGE, MASS.

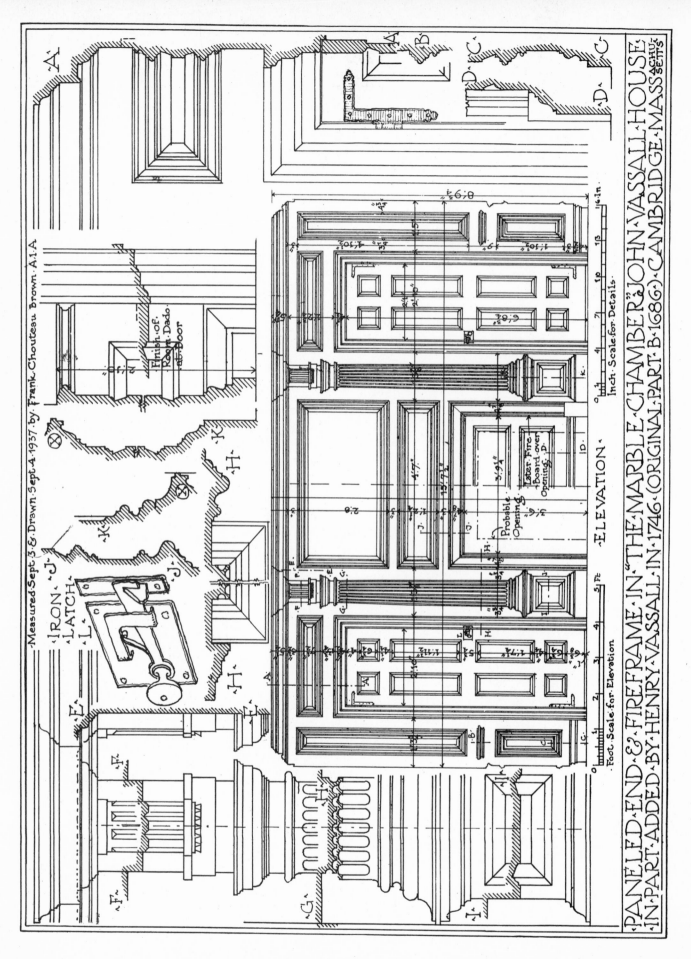

PANELED END & FIRE FRAME IN "THE MARBLE CHAMBER" JOHN VASSALL HOUSE
IN PART ADDED BY HENRY VASSALL IN 1746 (ORIGINAL PART B 1686) CAMBRIDGE MASSACHUSETTS

Measured Sept 3 & Drawn Sept 4 1937 by Frank Chouteau Brown A.I.A.

IRON LATCH

Finish of Room Dado at Door

Later Fire Board over Opening D

Probable Opening

ELEVATION

Inch Scale for Details

Foot Scale for Elevation

"THE MARBLE CHAMBER," 1746

HALL AND STAIRCASE IN PORTION ADDED BY MAJ. HENRY VASSALL IN 1746

THE JOHN VASSALL HOUSE—NO. 94 BRATTLE ST., CAMBRIDGE, MASSACHUSETTS
ORIGINAL WEST FRONT, ON HAWTHORN STREET, BEFORE 1686
REAR (EAST) PORTION ADDED BY MAJ. HENRY VASSALL IN 1746

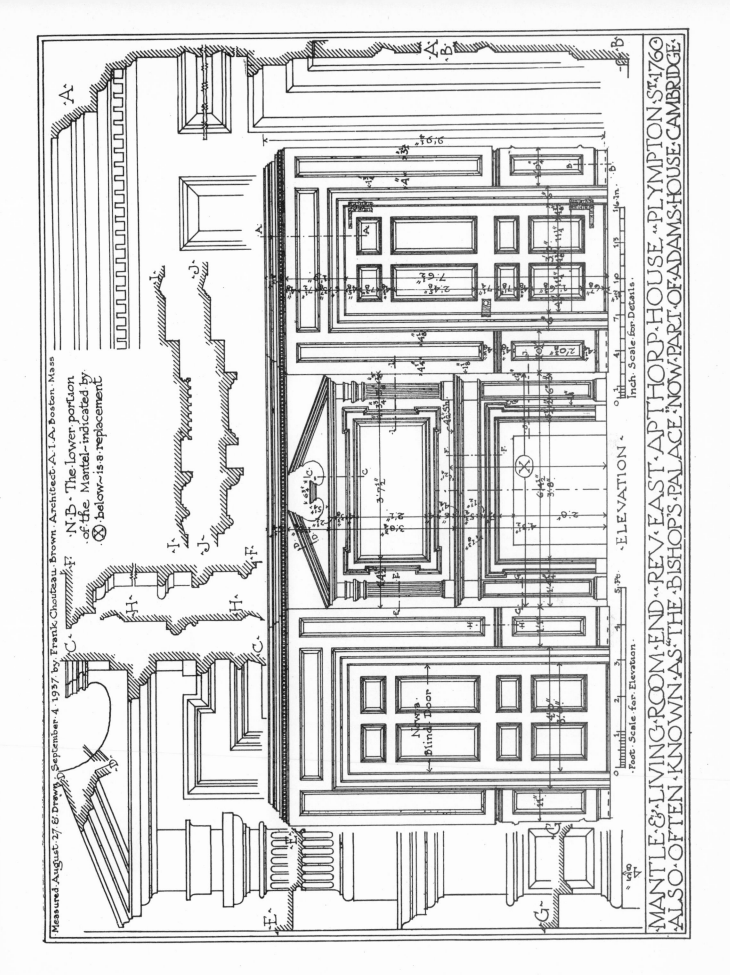

Measured. August. 27. & Drawn. September. 4. 1937. by. Frank. Chouteau. Brown. Architect. A. I. A. Boston. Mass

·N·B· The. lower. portion
.of. the. Mantel. indicated. by
⊗ below~ is. a. replacement

·ELEVATION·

Now ·a· Blind· Door

MANTLE·&·LIVING·ROOM·END·REV·EAST·APTHORP·HOUSE·"PLYMPTON·ST·1760·
·ALSO·OFTEN·KNOWN·AS·"THE·"BISHOP'S·PALACE"·NOW·PART·OF·ADAMS·HOUSE·CAMBRIDGE·

Foot· Scale· for· Elevation·

Inch· Scale· for· Details·

179

DETAIL OF MANTEL IN LIVING ROOM
APTHORP HOUSE—1761—NO. 15 PLYMPTON STREET, CAMBRIDGE, MASSACHUSETTS

ence, Governor of Massachusetts and Vice-President of the U. S. In 1818 it came into possession of Rev. Charles Lowell, pastor of the West Church, Boston (1806-1845), the father of James Russell Lowell.

The latter used as his Study the southwest room on the first floor until 1876, when he moved into the room in front of it, on the southeast corner of the house.

"The Larches" was built in 1808, and with its furnishings is one of the most beautiful of the Cambridge houses.

William Gray, who built the house, was Lieutenant Governor of the Commonwealth of Massachusetts in 1811,—at which time Elbridge Gerry was Governor and lived at "Elmwood," nearby.

The general style of the architecture is markedly similar to the houses of the noted Salem architect, Samuel McIntyre, especially in the delicacy of the over-doors and mantel pieces, for which McIntyre was justly famous. The Stair Hall wall paper is over one hundred years old, and the long parlor at the left, with its eight windows and two fireplaces, still maintains the atmosphere of the early years of the 19th century.

CHRIST CHURCH

Four meeting houses were in use in Cambridge before the present Christ Church was erected. The fourth edifice was "raised," Nov. 17, 1756, and the first service was held, July 24, 1757. It continued in use until 1833; but in 1759 a subscription was held for another church edifice in the town, and on October 15, 1761, the new Christ Church, Episcopal, was opened. Previously, Henry Vassall, Joseph Lee, John Vassall, Ralph Inman, Thomas Oliver, David Phips, Robert Temple, and James Apthorp had petitioned the English Society for the Propagation of the Gospel in Foreign Parts, to have a Church of England established in Cambridge, and the Rev. East Apthorp was appointed Missionary to Cambridge by that Society, in 1759. He had been born in Boston and had just graduated from Jesus College, Oxford, in Old England. Along with the first six petitioners named, he was made a member of the building Committee.

The committee agreed that the dimensions, including walls, but not chancel and tower, be sixty feet long by forty-five feet wide; that "the architect be at liberty to make any alteration in these dimensions, provided he does not enlarge the area"; that the building be of wood, with one tier of windows, and no gallery except an organ loft; that the cost not exceed £500 sterling; that Mr. Harrison, of Newport, be requested for "a plan and elevation of the outside and inside, and of the pulpit and vestry of the church, and if Mr. Harrison approves of it, there be no steeple, only a tower with a belfry; and that he be informed of the dimensions of a picture designed for the chancel." The dimensions of the building were adopted by the architect, Mr. Peter Harrison, who had also designed King's Chapel in Boston and the Redwood Library in Newport, but the cost ran to about £1300. The exterior, originally requested "to be of rough cast," was never applied. The church appears today much

FRONT HALL AND STAIRCASE DETAIL
VASSALL-CRAIGIE-LONGFELLOW HOUSE—1759,
CAMBRIDGE, MASSACHUSETTS

as it did then, except for the introduction of two bays, which added twenty-three feet to its length; but on the inside the hour-glass pulpit and box pews are gone.

Most of the church proprietors lived on Brattle Street; also known as "Tory Row" or "Church Lane," and had earlier belonged to King's Chapel in Boston. Disfavor was aroused by the beautiful and pretentious "Palace," built by the young rector for himself and wife near the College grounds. Both represented—to the other residents of the town—the power and ceremonial they had always associated with religion overseas and had come to this country to escape. Popular feeling ran high, and this opposition—headed by Dr. Mayhew, of the West Church in Boston—finally made the Rev. Apthorp's position so trying that he returned to England in 1764.

During the Revolution the building suffered badly. Its Tory congregation were all forced to leave with the British, and the church was closed—although there is a record that, on the last Sunday in 1775, the service was read at the request of Mrs. Washington, who had arrived December 11th; but Capt. Chester's company from Wethersfield, Conn., was quartered in the building, and melted window lights and organ pipes for bullets. After the army left, the church was again closed, but on June 19, 1778, a young officer of Burgoyne's Army who had died, was interred in the Vassall tomb beneath the church, and Americans plundered the building, destroyed the pulpit, reading desk, and communion table, and broke the bellows and pipes.

DETAILS OF DOORHEAD TREATMENTS

ENTRANCE FRONT, "THE LARCHES"—1808—22 LARCH ROAD, CAMBRIDGE, MASSACHUSETTS

Detail of Entrance

THE WOMEN'S CLUB HOUSE, TAUNTON, MASSACHUSETTS

Eastern Massachusetts

THE south eastern part of Massachusetts was in Colonial times one of the most closely settled and prosperous portions of the colonies, but since its industries were largely agricultural and mercantile, the population has for the most part not expanded with the rapidity that it has elsewhere, and there are in consequence many of the little towns which have much of the old work preserved.

New England was, of course, almost lacking in the resources both of power and materials which have produced the industrial cities in the United States. There was no coal, no ore, and comparatively little water power. Such industries as were built up in New England, as for example the shoe manufacturing plants at Lynn and the textile mills at New Bedford and Fall River, grew up principally because there was available a considerable amount of intelligent labor, although the raw materials came from a long way off. Such towns grew rapidly for a time and slowly thereafter and in them will be found little of the old American architecture. Providence, of course, while a comparatively large city and an important industrial center, has through some piece of good fortune preserved a number of its old houses and churches, but the surviving examples of early American architecture are for the most part to be found in the smaller and less industrial villages and towns, and the examples illustrated in this number came from Taunton, East Taunton, and Weymouth,—places of com-

paratively less importance now than they were one hundred years ago and which have grown apparently but little.

It is a never failing source of wonder that the Colonial times and the Colonial tradition immediately after the Declaration of Independence should have produced with such unfailing regularity work of so great an excellence. It seems to the student of the surviving examples as if perhaps never anywhere in the history of the world was there such a uniformly high standard of architecture as in the United States in 1800. There was practically no building of down right ugliness and there were a very great many of consummate beauty; the standards naturally varied in different parts of the United States, depending upon the amount of wealth available for development of the artistic impulses of the colonists, and also to a somewhat lesser extent upon the inborn aptitude for architectural expression which characterized the several races. It is perhaps impossible to say which was the more beautiful,—the architecture of South Carolina, that of Pennsylvania, of New Jersey, or of Southern New England, but each was certainly of a distinctive type, since each community established its own slight variation from the Georgian tradition; and while to the European all of our Colonial architecture looks more or less alike, the man who is familiar with it is readily able to distinguish between the solid, sturdy work of the Pennsylvanian, the more florid Carolinian, and the graceful and austere New England work. Of them all, perhaps, no other was so deep cut into the conscious-

DETAIL OF THE ARNOLD HOUSE,
WEYMOUTH, MASSACHUSETTS
Built during 1790

ness of the people as that of New England, which for nearly one hundred years persisted with comparatively slight differences, and even in the time of the Greek Revival, when all American architecture became nationalized, the local characteristics were maintained. It was preeminently a wooden architecture,—the proportion of the orders, of the openings, and of the cornices were distinctly that of wood, a point which can be nowhere better demonstrated than by the Arnold house at Weymouth, Massachusetts, in which a brick building is treated as if it were of wood. Consider the depth of the lintels in proportion to their span, or the treatment of the brick spandrel over the wooden Paladian window. It is obvious that the architect's sense of proportion was developed by wooden examples and not from previous knowledge of the requirements of brick construction; the lintels are probably heavy enough to carry the brick work above, but the brick carried by the Paladian window, even with the relieving arch over, is certainly not structurally sound. Imagine the English architect whose whole life had been devoted to building of brick, even a man whose delicacy of detail was so marked as that of Robert Adam, producing columns so slender as those of the porch of the Arnold house.

The New Englanders were certainly not noted for their light temperaments, and yet we find the Classic architecture of New England full of motives of the most playful description imaginable. Things which today we would regard as stunts were in those days apparently the ordinary habit of mind of the designer. Examine for a moment the photograph of the entrance doorway of the Women's Club at Taunton, Massachusetts in which the soffit of the raking cornice has been ornamented with a Chinese Chippendale motive and the return of the level cornice has been extended far enough toward the fan light to provide room for another and similar ornament. The designer probably felt that the space between the raking cornice and the fan light was too big to be left plain and while one would naturally expect a panelled treatment of some variety, here the architect has preferred to extend his cornice in a way, of which this is the sole example surviving, (if there were ever another one), and apparently the Chinese Chippendale ornament had sunk deeply into the mind of the designer since he repeated it at a bigger scale in the panel backs under the side lights.

Another unusual treatment of door head is that in the house at Taunton, Massachusetts. This is probably a comparatively late example although the method by

Detail of Entrance

A FARMHOUSE AT
EAST WEYMOUTH,
MASSACHUSETTS

Detail of Upper Part of Doorway
HOUSE AT TAUNTON, MASSACHUSETTS

which the narrow architrave of the door way turns up into a point over the side light was used in England in Jacobean times. This house, by the way, is a very good example of the manner in which the familiar pilaster treatment was often suggested rather than fully expressed. There is here no such thing as a full pilaster, nor a full entablature, and yet the structural significance of the order is admirably suggested.

Perhaps the handsomest of all the houses illustrated is the Deane-Barstow house in East Taunton, built in 1800. It is of excellent proportions with two admirable door ways. The whole character of the house seems to belie the date of construction which was the period in which the Greek Revival had begun to be the prevailing style throughout most of the country.

The farm house at East Weymouth, Massachusetts, is interesting because the English influence of the late Georgian period is clearly indicated. The house is perhaps not quite as happy in mass as many other examples of the same type and this to the modern architect is a somewhat consoling fact, since we today find it very easy to reproduce a Colonial house in every respect but one—its charm. Perhaps an analysis of the elements of this house at East Weymouth may help us to understand why the Colonial house which looks so simple to do with entire success is so very seldom successfully designed. The first important feature of the Colonial house is, of course, the proportion of the height from the ground to the lower side of the cornice to the length of the house. This house does not appear to differ from most Colonial houses in this respect, nor do many of the modern ones. The position of the chimneys and their size is another matter of considerable importance. It is obvious from this East Weymouth house that the placing of two chimneys at the ends or of a single one at the center is better than placing them as they are here, on center of the pairs of rooms at each end of the house; it is also obvious that these chimneys are both too square and too small. Another feature of this house in which it differs very slightly, but still it does differ from the typical Colonial house, is in the proportion of windows to wall, and also the fact that the openings on the first and second stories are of the same size. This is the proportion used in many of our modern houses, and is not the proportion used in the most successful of the Colonial houses. The Colonial windows were almost always smaller, with glass lights of a smaller size in relation to the entire facade. The second story windows here are placed very close to the cornice,—that is quite common in all Colonial houses, and less common in our houses of today, but there are good examples of Colonial work in which a considerable space intervenes between the window heads and the cornice. This house has wooden quoins on the corners and around the door, with clapboards of a very small exposure; another contributing element to the failure of this house to exhibit charm. The thing which to the writer is most important is the fact that the door way, delightful as it is in itself, is somewhat overscaled for the balance of the building, and as the elements which made up the composition of the Colonial house were so exceedingly few, a slight variation from the proper scale of any one of these elements will almost necessarily throw the whole composition out of unity. In this house the effect is not displeasing; it is rather unpleasing; and a precisely similar result is achieved by most of the modern attempts at recreation of the Colonial spirit.

The door way is in itself an exceedingly interesting illustration of the manner in which classic motives were modified in Colonial times. We find the orders treated with somewhat the same freedom by the Adam Brothers in English Georgian work. The carpenter architect of this building, probably following some book design, achieved a result which one would suppose to be only possible to the man who had a thorough mastery of the elements of architecture. Certain features of this door way indicate that its design was accidental rather than intentional, as for example; the heavy round molding

forming a sort of architrave, very distinctly overscaled as compared with the rest of the composition, the peculiar fret work or double dentil course forming the lower part of the cornice or the upper part of the frieze, and the fact that the consoles are not sure whether they are consoles or an additional dentil course, so far are they below the scale of Classic dentils and even below the scale of the order as a whole. It is interesting architecture rather than skillful design.

From the oldest to the latest of the houses illustrated a period of fifty years is covered and yet the character of the design has changed in an almost imperceptible way. The tradition of this part of New England, the first to be settled, was early established and little changed. With the exception of the Arnold house there is nothing very striking or magnificent about any of the buildings. They were apparently the typical "run of the mill" of Colonial days and yet their charm, their delicacy of proportion. and ease in composition is almost impossible for the twentieth century architect to duplicate without making an exact reproduction of one of the original sources. There was a mastery of the simple stylistic materials of that time in the hands of every carpenter, because it must be assumed that most of these houses were built without formal plans. The excellence of the Colonial mechanics in design as well as in execution is the architectural marvel of the eighteenth century.

HOUSE AT
TAUNTON,
MASSACHUSETTS

*Detail of Cornice,
Caps, Etc.*

HOUSE AT
TAUNTON,
MASSACHUSETTS

NOW USED
AS THE
WOMEN'S
CLUB

The DEANE–BARSTOW HOUSE
EAST TAUNTON, MASSACHUSETTS

MEASURED DRAWINGS *from*
The George F. Lindsay Collection

ELEVATION·OF·SIDE·DOORWAY.
Scale 1/2"=1'-0"

SIDE·ELEV.
FRONT·DOOR

ELEVATION·OF·
S

GRADE LINE

THE · DEANE · B
EAST · TAUNTON

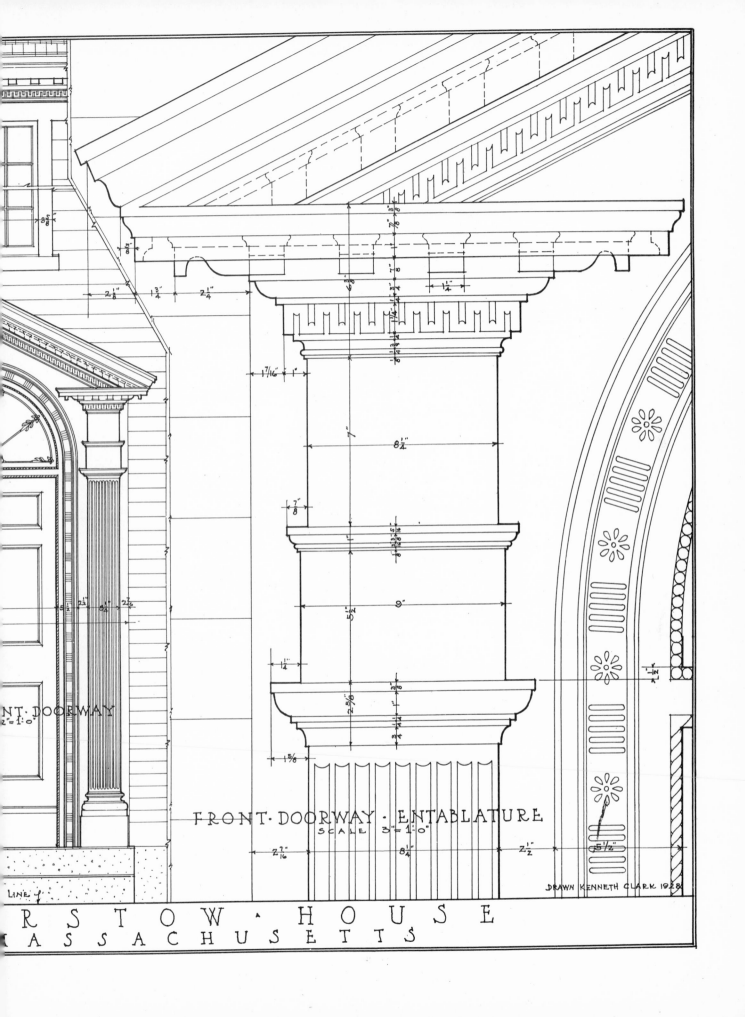

NT·DOORWAY
2"=1'-0"

FRONT·DOORWAY·ENTABLATURE
SCALE 3"=1'-0"

DRAWN KENNETH CLARK 1928

RSTOW · HOUSE
ASSACHUSETTS

LINE

The Side Door

THE DEANE–BARSTOW HOUSE, EAST TAUNTON, MASSACHUSETTS

*Detail of Upper Part
of Side Doorway*

195

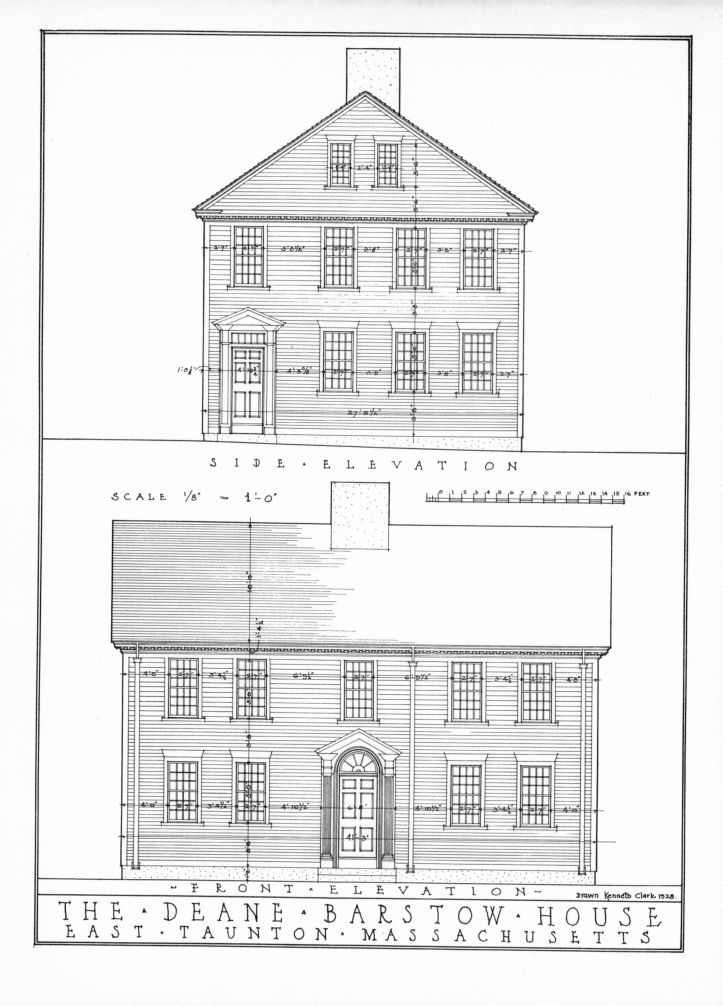

SIDE · ELEVATION

SCALE 1/8" = 1'-0"   0 1 2 3 4 5 6 7 8 9 10 11 12 13 14 15 16 FEET

~ FRONT · ELEVATION ~   Drawn Kenneth Clark 1928.

THE · DEANE · BARSTOW · HOUSE
EAST · TAUNTON · MASSACHUSETTS

The Front Door

*Detail of Upper Part
of Front Doorway*

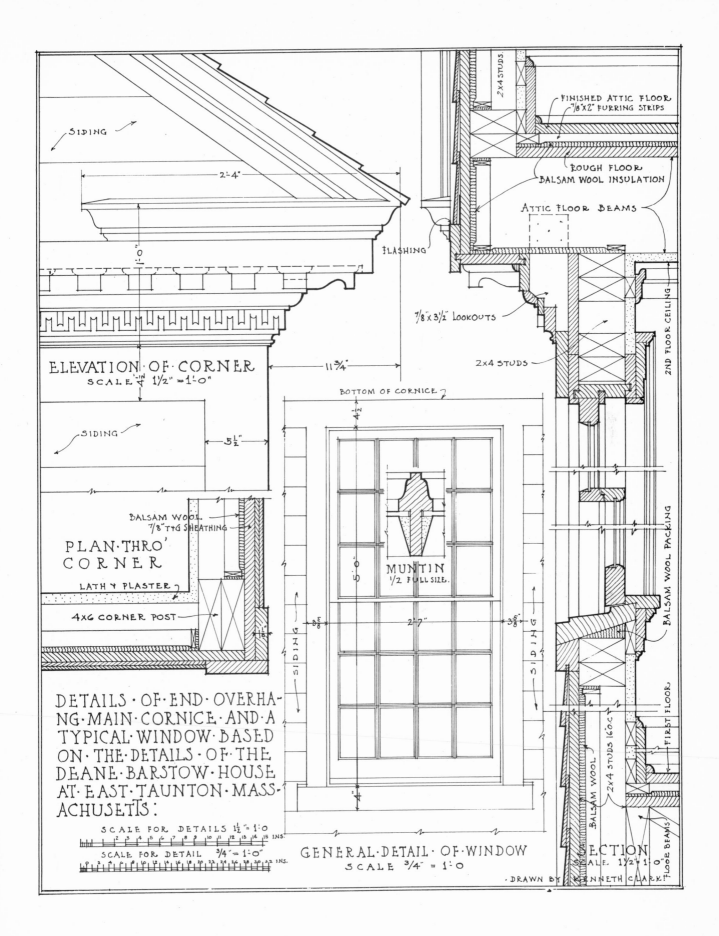

SIDING

2'-4"

FLASHING

ELEVATION·OF·CORNER
SCALE 1½" = 1'-0"

SIDING

5½"

BALSAM WOOL
7/8" T+G SHEATHING

PLAN·THRO'
CORNER

LATH Y PLASTER

4x6 CORNER POST

DETAILS·OF·END·OVERHA-
NG·MAIN·CORNICE·AND·A
TYPICAL·WINDOW·BASED
ON·THE·DETAILS·OF·THE
DEANE·BARSTOW·HOUSE
AT·EAST·TAUNTON·MASS-
ACHUSETTS·

SCALE FOR DETAILS 1½" = 1'-0"
SCALE FOR DETAIL 3/4" = 1'-0"

11¾"

BOTTOM OF CORNICE

MUNTIN
½ FULL SIZE.

3/8"   2'-7"   3/8"

SIDING   SIDING

5'-0"

GENERAL·DETAIL·OF·WINDOW
SCALE 3/4" = 1'-0"

2X4 STUDS.

FINISHED ATTIC FLOOR
7/8"X2" FURRING STRIPS

ROUGH FLOOR
BALSAM WOOL INSULATION

ATTIC FLOOR BEAMS

7/8" X 3½" LOOKOUTS

2X4 STUDS

2ND FLOOR CEILING

BALSAM WOOL PACKING

BALSAM WOOL

FIRST FLOOR

2X4 STUDS 16"O.C.

FLOOR BEAMS

SECTION
SCALE 1½" = 1'-0"

·DRAWN·BY·KENNETH·CLARK·

199

MOUNT VERNON MANSION

The hip roof is especially appropriate to a house of this size.

Early American Roofs

THE roofs are so important a feature of Colonial houses that the various types are often distinguished by names describing their roof shapes, but nobody ever has much to say about them, and few modern houses of Colonial precedent employ anything but the straight gable, or the gambrel roof. Our ancestors were more fluent designers than are we; problems of grade and symmetry which to us are insurmountable seemingly presented no problems to them, and where we content ourselves with the simplest of roof forms they used a multitude of types, sometimes for definite reasons—more often, perhaps, just because they liked them.

It is worth while to examine the sketches below just to see how great was the number of their varieties. Amusing names, some of them, calling up the circumstances under which they were built; the common household objects which inspired the forms, or the laws (either enacted or economic) which dictated the methods of roofing adopted by the farmers and sailors who formed so great a proportion of our early housewrights.

There is a word which is not used, but should not be forgotten; we still have ship-wrights and wheel-wrights by name, but instead of house-wrights we have carpenters and cabinetmakers; even "joiners" has come to apply to a collector of societies, rather than

a branch of house carpentry; the legal profession holds its old terms and lawyers are still "Attorneys and Counsellors at Law" while the "Carpenter and Joiner" of the eighteen-sixties is now only the man behind the sign "Jobbing Done."

We will some day, it may be supposed, give up all our pitched roofs, be they steep or flat or gambrel, and roof our houses with flat slabs of waterproof concrete, or some new processed metal which will not shrink or split as it adapts itself to the hot sun of our long summers or the biting cold of our February nights; but when this occurs, and a pitched roof becomes to our descendants as fantastic as battlements on a stucco cottage, not only will we have lost one of our traditional habits of life, but our northern landscape will have lost the most picturesque accent (next to the church spires) which it possesses.

The house with the flat roof is not necessarily ugly or even unpicturesque; there are plenty of houses in Tunis and Spain and Guatemala to prove that the flat-roofed house may have a charm and beauty all its own; but beneath our northern skies, within our landscape, we must have roofs that show. Take, for example, the little picture at the head of page 204, showing the Quarters and Shops of Mount Vernon, the small clean white houses with their simple roofs marching along against the foliage of the great trees

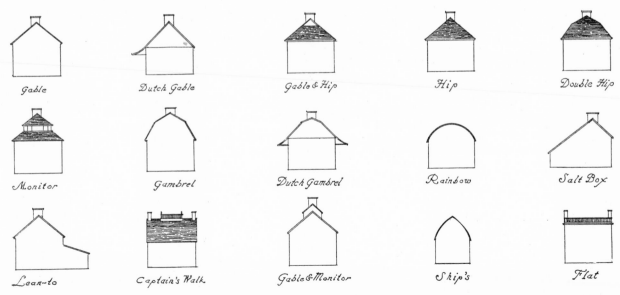

Gable   Dutch Gable   Gable & Hip   Hip   Double Hip

Monitor   Gambrel   Dutch Gambrel   Rainbow   Salt Box

Lean-to   Captain's Walk   Gable & Monitor   Ship's   Flat

201

THE PRINCE HOUSE, FLUSHING, NEW YORK
A gambrel and gable roof used on a late 18th Century house.

A 1757 HOUSE, EAST GREENWICH, RHODE ISLAND
Another example of the gable on hip roof—this time with a window.

GOVERNOR TRUMBULL HOUSE, LEBANON, CONNECTICUT, BUILT 1753
A hip roof with short ridge.

THE WITTER HOUSE, CHAPLIN, CONNECTICUT, BUILT 1828
Early type of monitor used on house of later date.

OUTBUILDINGS OF MOUNT VERNON MANSION

Simple gable roofs are perfectly suited to these small structures.

full of little holes for the sky to peer through. Not only in this picture, but in reality, they are of breathtaking beauty, not because of any wealth of carving or delicacy of design, but because the simple masses of these early buildings attained once and for all a perfect attunement to our American scene. No one can do a better Parthenon; it is the perfect solution of a simple architectural problem in the Grecian setting, and there is nothing more perfect than perfection. So with our early American work, by some happy accident, or by the expression of obscure instinct, our forefathers achieved in these small white Colonial houses nestling in the shelter of great trees, an absolute rightness which cannot be improved.

Yet, just as in Greece there are other buildings than the Parthenon which are in their ways just as beautiful—the Ionic Column is unlike but parallel to the Doric—so in our Colonial houses there were many roof forms, each of which in its proper setting satisfies our æsthetic requirements—and the Colonial designers seem to have felt about them much as we do. On the flat bare plains of Long Island and the wind-swept open seaside dunes, they rarely erected the prim, demurely stately, two-story house of the villages. We find on Long Island the "salt-box" and the "lean-to," in Jersey and along the Down East coast the "gambrel" or "rainbow," types rarely seen in villages, except for the modification of the gambrel used by the Dutch around New York. The hip roof was the hardest to frame and only shows to advantage on buildings of considerable size. Perhaps for these reasons we find it used only on those houses where dignity, or at

least the pretense of it, was desired. The straight gable roof is apt to be over-dominant on the big house, and very likely it was this that caused the main building of Mount Vernon to be built with a hip roof, while the smaller outbuildings have, for the most part, gable ends.

Neither the material of the body of the house nor the part of the country in which it was built appears to have had much influence on the choice of roof design; we find wood, brick, and stone houses with hip roofs and gable roofs; we find hip roofs, gable roofs, and gambrel roofs in New England, around New York, and in the South; apparently the builders in all the Colonies knew what was being done in roofs, even if they didn't know how they were built; and there is occasional internal evidence that the builders started a roof of some peculiar form without knowing just how it was to be completed, and finished it by the light of pure reason, rather than by the lamp of experience.

There was, however, a strong local flavor in the design of roofs, just as there was in the choice of scale of ornament; the gambrel of New England was composed of different pitches from that of Maryland, the Pennsylvania gable roof (there much the most popular type) had different relations of height and breadth from those in Massachusetts and Virginia, although, curiously enough, the Pennsylvanians arrived at gable ends of almost exactly the shape common on the eastern end of Long Island; the New England roofs were less steep and the Southern ones steeper. That variance was most likely temperamental, since the greatest difficulty in the way of making a roof tight was snow, and snow is supposed to be more common —one might almost say more prevalent—in New England than in Carolina.

Construction also influenced roof shape, although construction was often more influenced by tradition and desire than by economic factors. In New Jersey for example, the Dutch settlers used much stone; and although stone has been discovered in New England, stone houses have not ("What, never?" "Well, hardly ever!") and although lime was scarce and dear in New Jersey, the Dutchman built of stone just the same; for mortar he used mud. Mud is not hydraulic; so they

NORTON HOUSE, GUILFORD, CONNECTICUT
Built circa *1690.*

protected these mud-built houses by wide overhanging roofs, and to get the overhang they swept the eaves out in great curves, producing roof lines of real grace and charm, and almost impossible to ventilate, so that the second stories of these Dutch houses were too hot to sleep in. Papa and Mamma slept on the ground floor, while the children stayed awake on the second.

One style of roof only was peculiar to a single section—the monitor roof to New England. Beginning perhaps as a double-hip roof—a sort of hipped gambrel—it was found easier to make the junction between the two pitches tight

SPENCER-PIERCE HOUSE, NEWBURY, MASSACHUSETTS, BUILT 1650
The straight gable roof on an unusual house suggestive of an earlier English prototype.

THE CAPTAIN JOHN CLARK HOUSE, SOUTH CANTERBURY, CONNECTICUT

Built in 1732, enlarged about 1790.   Gable on hip roof to receive chimney.

THE CHAMPION HOUSE, EAST HADDAM, CONNECTICUT, BUILT 1794

A hip roof so flat that a balustrade appears to be necessary.

if a vertical board were introduced between them: such a board can be seen on the roof of the Prince House or in a gable-on-hip roof below it. Then perhaps some bright young man bethought himself that if this were raised a foot or two, there would be space for air and light; and behold! the monitor roof. Sometimes this object was accomplished by a superimposed gable, or by running the ridge of a hipped roof out beyond the structural hip and putting in a window, giving the gable-on-hip roof; sometimes it was flattened and a captain's walk built; and sometimes a general amalgamation of monitor, cupola, and captain's walk resulted in a sort of enclosed bridge deck as in the house at Lyme, New Hampshire.

farmers. One would have expected the opposite, since our much greater variety of materials makes very simple the problems that must have sorely puzzled our ancestors. The average Colonial house was roofed with shingles; a few in Pennsylvania and the Vermont-New York line with slate; a very few with metal, lead, or at the end of the period, tin-plated iron. Lead, for many years the only material available for flashing, was beaten out by hand with small sheets and was enormously expensive, so that flashing was very sparingly used and in many houses was absent altogether. Our modern builders would certainly be puzzled if asked to make a roof tight without it, and most carpenters would rebel if asked to shingle a roof

THE MORRIS-PURDEE HOUSE, MORRIS COVE, NEW HAVEN, CONNECTICUT
In 1670, architects did not feel it necessary to receive minor roofs directly on major ones.

Nor have we gone further than they; perhaps, on the contrary, we have retrogressed, if by retrogression we mean a failure to exploit the available possibilities. As was said above we commonly use three forms of roof only, the gable, gambrel, and hip; the more complicated forms involving curves, such as the ship, rainbow, and Dutch, rarely appear, if we except the state-designed barns and silos built by our progressive

with a pitch of 15°, or a rainbow roof, and make it watertight. One trick of the older builders we are beginning to use again, that of canting the ridge lines at the chimneys, was originally a trick to shed water from the chimneys, but is now done to soften roof lines.

Much of our modern "Colonial" work is hard, wiry, correct, and dull; greater variety in roof lines is essential to improvement in this respect.

REAR PORCH, GUNSTON HALL, FAIRFAX COUNTY, VIRGINIA, BUILT 1758

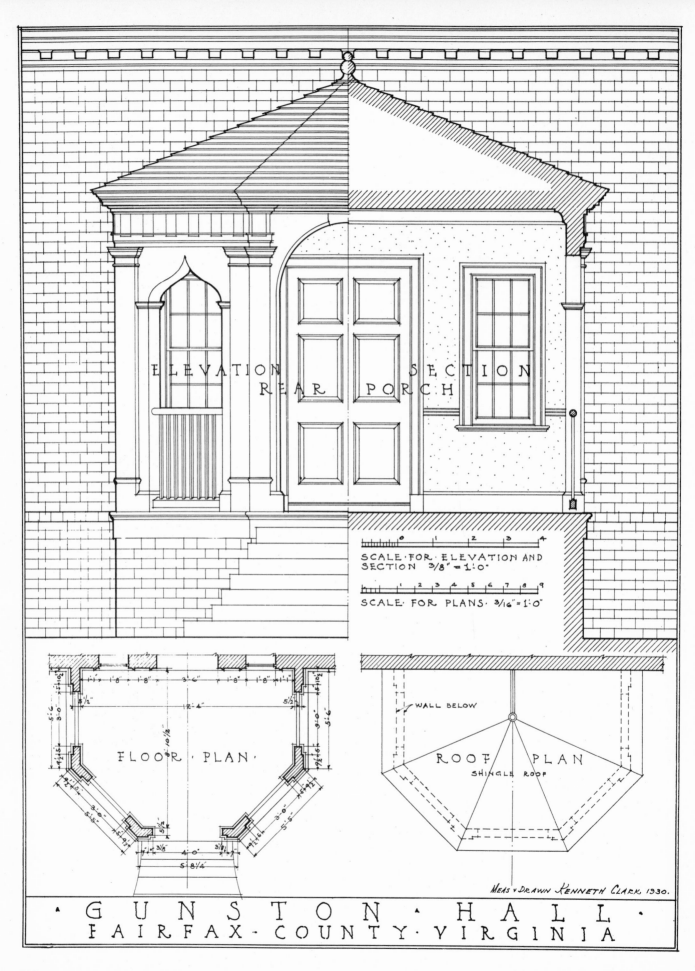

ELEVATION   SECTION
R E A R   P O R C H

SCALE·FOR·ELEVATION·AND
SECTION· 3/8"= 1'-0"

SCALE·FOR·PLANS· 3/16"= 1'-0"

FLOOR · PLAN ·

WALL BELOW

R O O F   P L A N
SHINGLE· ROOF

MEAS·&·DRAWN KENNETH CLARK 1930.

· G U N S T O N · H A L L ·
F A I R F A X · C O U N T Y · V I R G I N I A

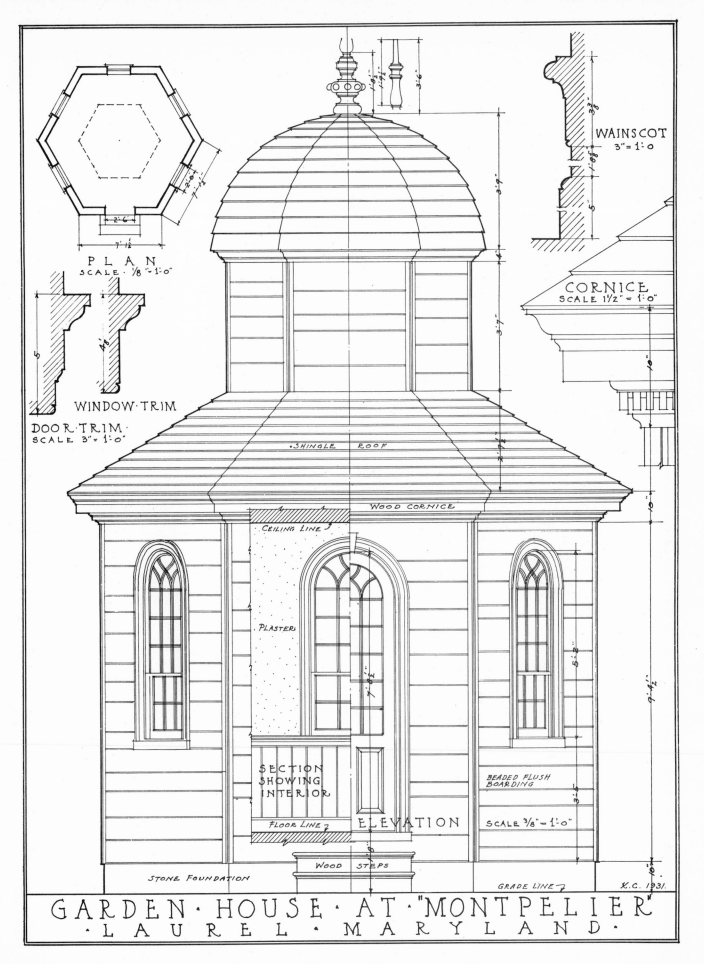

PLAN
SCALE · 1/8" = 1'-0"

WINDOW·TRIM

DOOR·TRIM
SCALE 3" = 1'-0"

WAINSCOT
3" = 1'-0"

CORNICE
SCALE 1½" = 1'-0"

·SHINGLE   ROOF

WOOD CORNICE

CEILING LINE

PLASTER

SECTION
SHOWING
INTERIOR

FLOOR LINE

ELEVATION

BEADED FLUSH
BOARDING

SCALE 3/8" = 1'-0"

STONE FOUNDATION

WOOD STEPS

GRADE LINE

K.C. 1931.

GARDEN·HOUSE·AT·"MONTPELIER
·LAUREL·MARYLAND·

211

GARDEN HOUSE, MONTPELIER, LAUREL, MARYLAND

THE DYCKMAN HOUSE, NEW YORK, N. Y., BUILT 1787

THE JOHN P. B. WESTERVELT HOUSE, CRESKILL, NEW JERSEY

*Main house built with mud mortar, needing protection on gable
end. Addition built with lime mortar and gable end unprotected.*

URN AND FENCE POST, THE PIERCE—NICHOLS HOUSE, SALEM, MASSACHUSETTS,
Built in 1782. Samuel McIntyre, Architect

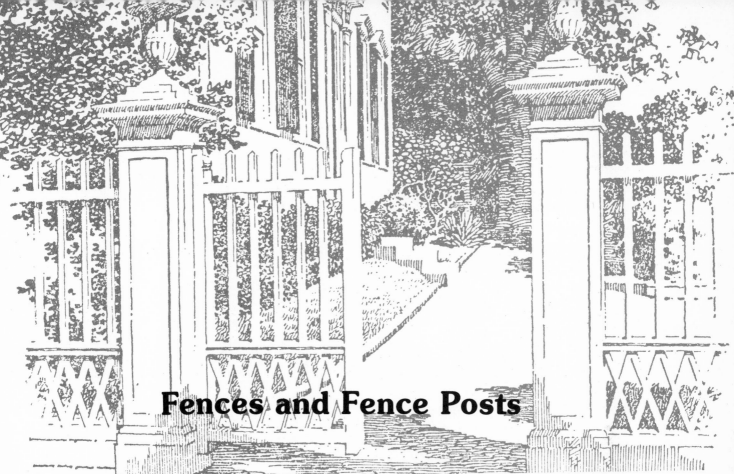

Fences and Fence Posts

Once upon a time, when our ancestors spoke of their "defences," they referred to the great walls and battlements which protected them against their warlike neighbors; but, nowadays our neighbors are more neighborly, and the "defences" have dwindled down to "fences." The evolution of the fence has proceeded in accordance with the nature of the marauders to be shut out; the utmost that is required of a fence in this day and country is a stout resistance to little boys, cows or chickens.

The tall solid masonry walls of the Continental estate are not friendly in America, nor are they desirable or necessary here, where we have endless land and comparatively little population. The impulse for privacy on the part of the well-to-do is just as insistent today as ever, or the owner of a newly bought piece of property would not rush into an architect's office and ask for something arresting in the way of fence design. In crowded Europe, however, the solid wall was frequently the only thing which gave privacy, but for America I have always felt, that, as a general principle, a fence which was not absolutely necessary had better be done away with altogether, although, if the conditions actually required such protection, it should not obstruct the landscape, but rather give the passerby as extended a view of Nature's loveliness as is possible. It is astonishing, where, in a rocky country, the farmers have laid the stones into many fences, how much these barriers interfere with the view of the

FENCE DETAIL
House in Newburyport, Massachusetts

landscape. To prove the statement, it is necessary only to take down these criscross scars on the green-sward, as the author has done many times, to see how the view is opened up thereby, and how the land leaps out in acreage before you. Even on an estate's outside edge, I have always resented the intrusion of a high stone fence as being unfriendly and unneighborly, and usually, I find, that it is better manners and better architecture to do away with such unsightly obstructions. The traveller in Spain will see the gigantic cactus frequently planted in rows as a fence, and it makes a

FENCEPOST, NEWBURYPORT, MASSACHUSETTS

decidedly effective barrier. We have varieties of thorns which will do equally well and in fact the whole idea of using planting as a means of designating boundaries or creating barriers is an ingratiating one, and we hope our *confrères*, the landscape architects, may take it up and develop it. As for ourselves, we have not been very much encouraged by the way the suggestion has been received by the laity. Iron, stone or wood as a material are what drift into the mind of the average man when he is inspired by the thought that the time has come when he must begin to build fences.

FENCE OF THE HAVEN HOUSE, PORTSMOUTH, NEW HAMPSHIRE

THE JUDGE HAYES' HOUSE AND FENCE, SOUTH BERWICK, MAINE

FENCE AND FENCE POSTS IN NEWBURYPORT, MASSACHUSETTS

Let us try to adjust our imaginations to how engaging life may have been in the pleasant town of Salem, as depicted by the photograph of Chestnut Street. Here we have fence design in its most beautiful and appropriate flowering. Here are privacy and a proper regard for one's neighbors, expressed in faultless fashion.

What is true of Chestnut Street, Salem, is also true of High Street in Newburyport. In both of these Massachusetts towns the fence is often an integral part of the approach,

Nothing could be better architecture than the types of fence and fence posts shown in the illustrations on pages five, six and seven. What could be more in keeping than the old house and the fence at Laurel, Long Island, illustrated on page three, though the gateposts have a strong suspicion of the influence of the Victorian Era? This is the simplest type of fence conceivable, but it is

FENCE POST, NEWBURYPORT, MASSACHUSETTS

CHESTNUT STREET FROM NO. 10, LOOKING WEST, SALEM, MASSACHUSETTS

FENCE AND FENCE POSTS, THE WENTWORTH HOUSE, PORTSMOUTH, NEW HAMPSHIRE

SALEM AND
NEWBURY PORT
FENCE POSTS
AND URNS

good American architecture, nevertheless, and we cannot help calling attention to Nature's most delightful bit of architecture, shown in the branches of the old apple tree in the foreground.

For a perfect example of a Colonial fence, we call attention to the illustration showing the fence in front of the Loring-Emmerton House, Salem, Massachusetts. The pickets are exactly right in size, and it is easy for the architect to imagine how much heavier they would be had they been left to modern draughting room methods of detailing. The whole design is of absorbing interest in showing how every part has been treated to conform to the designer's feeling for lightness and grace. Perhaps his thought was to obstruct the view of the landscape as little as possible; at any rate, here is an old-time essay which well illustrates the general principles enunciated above. The horizontal rails of the fence have been moulded, to lighten their effect, and the base has been kept low. The detail of the post is delicate and refined, and the urn on the top is perhaps the only feature which needs to be reduced in the scale of its ornamentation, but that only very slightly.

A type of fence which is both effective and always satisfactory for use as a street boundary is the one on High Street, Newburyport, Massachusetts, frequently repeated in present-day fences, but often the fine proportions of the old-time one are lost, because the modern tendency is to make it all too heavy.

In the old fence in front of the Wentworth House, Portsmouth, is a combination of open and the closed fence, that in regard to the solid portion, we are quite willing to withdraw what we have written about obscuring the landscape and being unneighborly. Let us hope that something unseemly is kept from the public view, in which case we can stick to our principles, without being embarrassed by having to admit an exception.

The gateway, shown at Farmington, Connecticut, built about 1790, is very effectively and unusually well designed and would lend itself particularly well to garden gate design, rather than as precedent for a main entrance gate; although here it serves its aesthetic and practical purpose well.

At Stamford, Connecticut, and at Vergennes, Vermont, we have fencing which is more similar to modern methods of design, and the increased weight of the parts is not to its advantage, though the fence posts are well done.

In the picture of the fence and gateway of the "King" Caesar House, at Duxbury, Massachusetts, is shown a simple, usual and effective way of accentuating the entrance, by main posts at the corners, between which is a semi-circular fencing, with the smaller gate posts between them. In the present instance, however, the urns, while generally in keeping, may possibly be revised copies of excellent originals.

The fence of Judge Hayes' House, South Berwick, accentuates the posts by keeping the fencing between them very light. The elevated position of the house on the terrace, the garden spot to the right, are all very attractive and very typical of the hill country, and the house shown is a distinctive example of architecture and planting as exemplified in the American home.

We are happy to draw to a conclusion in the contemplation of so much good taste as was shown by the early craftsman who built this house in Maine, and we do so with an earnest appeal to those interested in early American architecture—White Pine architecture, if you will,—for it was that—to study this illustration well. Here is the perfect piece of architecture which our vainglorious friend is going to build on his newly acquired parcel of real estate, but never does, and I will venture the statement, as a fact, that this owner did not commence his home-building by surrounding the vacant property with the finely designed fence which has called forth our approbation!

No—by no means did the Colonial architect do his work in that back handed manner. The fence that surrounded the house or at least that shut it off from too direct contact with every casual passerby on the street must have been more than a mere inconsequential detail to him.

It must have been, I have always felt, quite as important a part of the entire design as the entrance doorway, the interior panelling or the exquisitely designed window frames that the Colonial architect used whenever the opportunity presented itself.

GATEWAY
House Near Stamford, Connecticut

GATEPOSTS AND GATE, THE H. K. OLIVER HOUSE, SALEM, MASSACHUSETTS, BUILT ABOUT 1799
The Urns and Gateposts were originally part of the palatial home constructed by the mariner, Elias H. Derby.

GATEWAY AND FENCE, HOME OF JAMES RUSSELL LOWELL, CAMBRIDGE, MASSACHUSETTS

HOUSE ON OUTSKIRTS OF BOSTON, MASSACHUSETTS

328 ESSEX STREET, SALEM, MASSACHUSETTS

FENCE AND GATEWAY—THE "KING" CAESAR HOUSE, DUXBURY, MASSACHUSETTS

FENCE OF THE LEWIS HOUSE, BROOKFIELD, MASSACHUSETTS

ENTRANCE GATEWAY
The Admiral Cowles House, Farmington, Connecticut

SALEM AND NEWBURYPORT
FENCE POSTS AND URNS